THE LOVE OF
MOTORCYCLING

THE LOVE OF
MOTORCYCLING

Graham Forsdyke

OCTOPUS

CONTENTS

First published 1977 by
Octopus Books Limited
59 Grosvenor Street, London W1

© 1977 Octopus Books Limited
ISBN 0 7064 0601 X

Produced by Mandarin Publishers Limited
22a Westlands Road, Quarry Bay, Hong Kong
Printed in Hong Kong

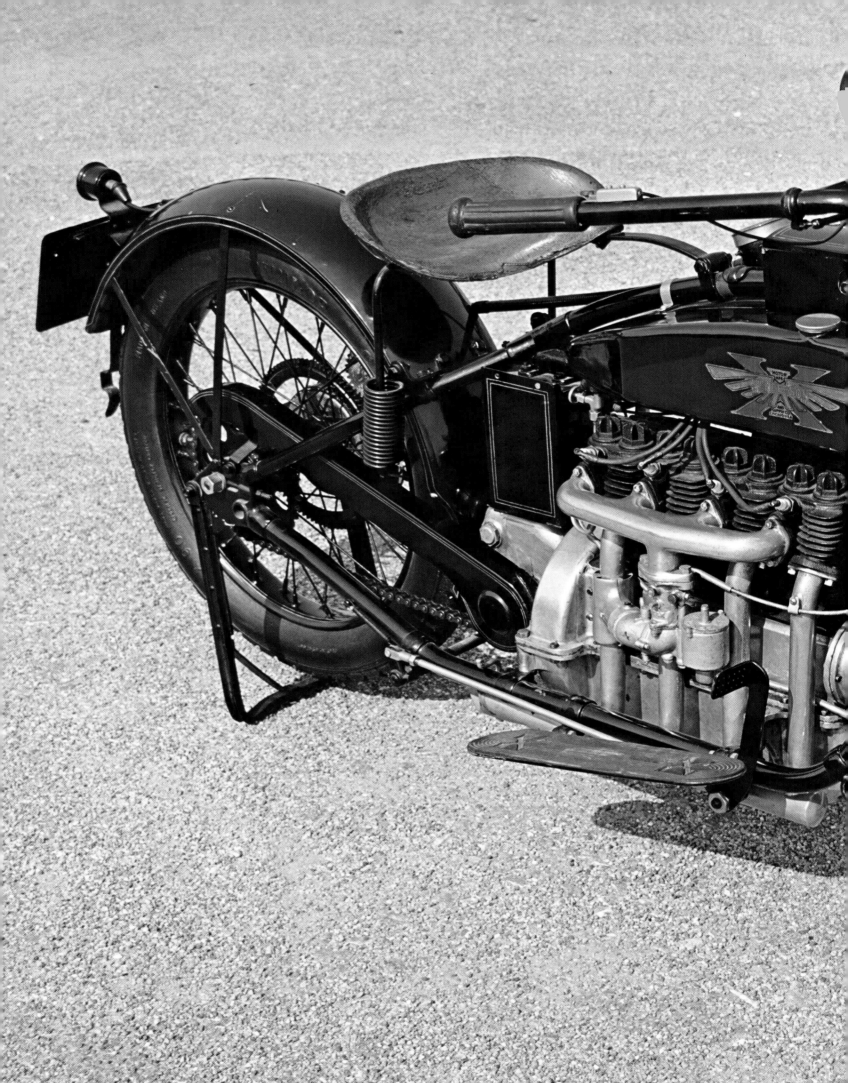

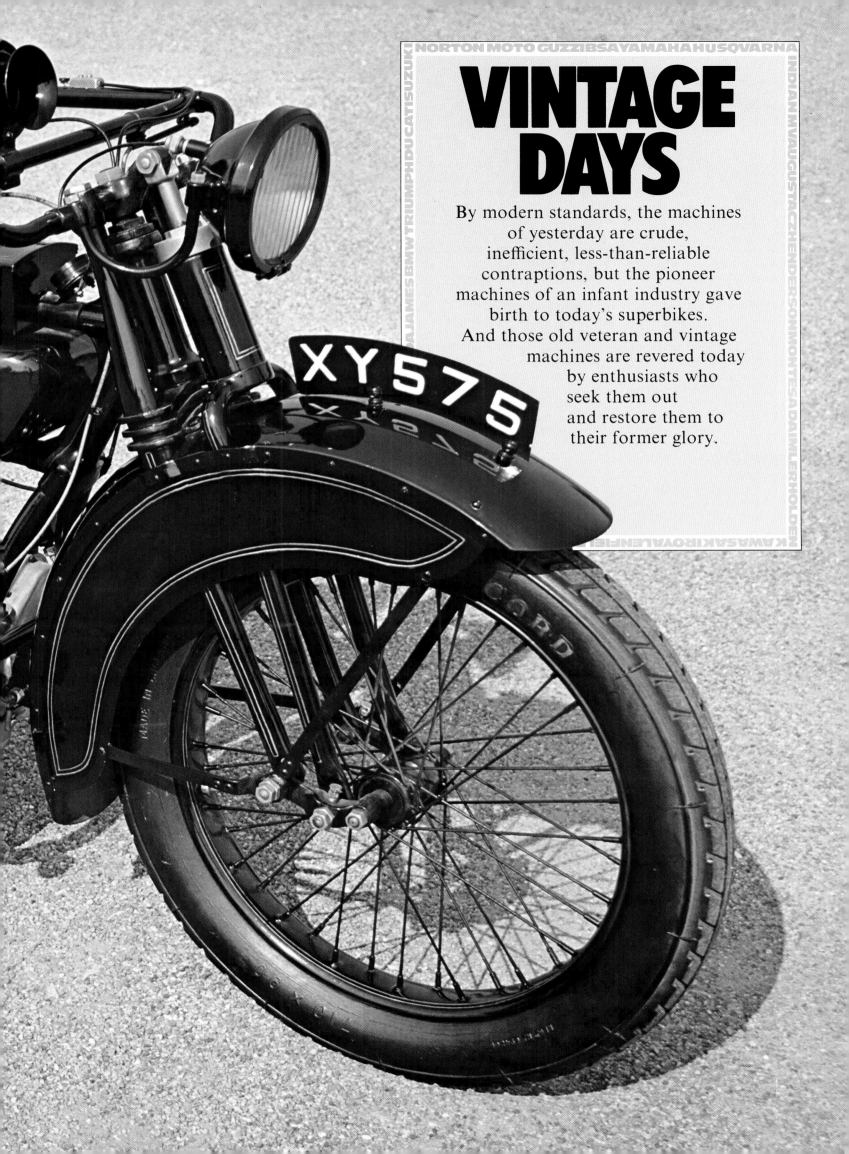

VINTAGE DAYS

By modern standards, the machines
of yesterday are crude,
inefficient, less-than-reliable
contraptions, but the pioneer
machines of an infant industry gave
birth to today's superbikes.
And those old veteran and vintage
machines are revered today
by enthusiasts who
seek them out
and restore them to
their former glory.

XY 575

From the dawn of time, man has had the urge to travel farther and faster than his own God-given legs could carry him. For many centuries he could accomplish this only with the co-operation of the friendly horse or camel. Animal power had its limitations, though. So did the steam railway, which opened to passenger service in the first quarter of the 19th century. True, the railway did get people from place to place quickly – but it was not personal transport. The bicycle proved a different matter. Here at last was something that made man individually mobile yet required no costly feeding or stabling. However, the bicycle's speed and endurance were limited by the rider's own muscle power. Motorcycles were to bypass this barrier.

As early as 1869 an adventurous Frenchman managed to fit a light Perreaux single-cylinder steam engine to a cycle frame and, for the first time, went for a spin under mechanical power. In the next decade or so, various other experimenters applied steam power to bicycles and tricycles. In America, a gentleman named Lucius D. Copeland even went into production in a modest way with a steam-driven pennyfarthing. But as we now know, the steam bicycle was a dead-end line of investigation, too cumbersome and too complicated to be a practical proposition. Although the world didn't know it, motorized transport was awaiting the arrival of the relatively light and high-speed internal-combustion engine.

By general assent, Gottlieb Daimler is credited with the title of 'father of the industry', though in fact the British inventor Edward Butler was working along similar lines to Daimler at about the same time. Butler's drawings of a rear-wheel-driven three-wheeler (he called it the Petrolcycle) were exhibited at the Stanley Show of 1884, the same year in which he was granted Provisional Patent Number 13541. A year later, his tricycle was on the road. Daimler, too, was in the field in 1885, with a wooden-frame device looking more like a clothes-horse than a motorcycle. Its four-stroke, single-cylinder engine operating on the Otto principle, drove the rear wheel through a flat belt and spur gearing. Daimler's assistant, Wilhelm Maybach, reputedly rode the unwieldy vehicle a distance of 16 kilometres (10 miles). But, in truth, Daimler's machine was no more than a means to an end. Having proved to his own satisfaction that an internal-combustion engine could be employed in a self-propelled vehicle, he abandoned motorcycles and devoted his research entirely to cars.

Not until 10 years later did things begin to happen in the two-wheel world. Then, in 1895, emerged three independent items of significance. In Germany, two mechanics named Hildebrand and Wolfmuller abandoned experiments with steam power for their light, multi-tube frame cycle and switched instead to a two-cylinder petrol engine. In France, the aristocratic Count de Dion had been trying the effect of a steam engine on a pedal tricycle without getting anywhere; now he, too, turned to a petrol engine. And in England, Colonel Holden (later Sir Henry Capel Holden) began to develop a motorcycle with two double-ended horizontal cylinders; Holden's four, like the Hildebrand and Wolfmuller twin, drove directly onto the rear axle.

All three were to go into production, and the Hildebrand and Wolfmuller is generally acclaimed as the first commercially successful motorcycle. Interestingly, there was no flywheel, and rubber straps were used at each side to assist in returning the piston during the compression stroke. The cylinders were water cooled, the water being carried in a curved tank that served, also, as the rear mudguard.

Count Albert de Dion and his partner, Georges Bouton, had been experimenting with steam tricycles since 1887, and it was again a tricycle which was the object of their attention in 1895, with a small petrol engine developing $\frac{1}{2}$ bhp at the then unprecedented shaft speed of 1,500 rpm; this early De Dion Bouton was, also, the first to house its flywheels within the crankcase.

From then on, a whole range of De Dion Bouton engines came into being (including in 1898, power units for the Santos-Dumont airship), and production of De Dion engines, motor cycles and tricycles spread from France, under licence, to England, Belgium, and even America.

They were raced, not only in cyclodromes but also in the town-

Previous pages: Fitted with a reverse gear as well as three forward gears, the 1,301 cc Henderson with its side-valve, four-cylinder engine was a natural for sidecar work. The machines were produced in America from 1911 until the factory's demise 20 years later.

Far left: The machine that started it all – the 'wooden wonder' Daimler produced in 1885. Two additional outrigger wheels kept the machine upright.

Left: Clean lines were the hallmark of Royal Enfield machines produced in England in the 1920s. The company's history dated back to 1900.

Below: Typical of the big tourers produced in America, this vee-twin Harley-Davidson is of 1915 vintage.

to-town dashes popular at the close of the 19th century, and one De Dion trike is recorded as winning the 1896 Paris-Marseilles-Paris race at an average speed of 23.3 km/h (14.5 mph). Two years later, another won the Paris-Bordeaux-Paris at 45 km/h (28 mph).

By that time, however, De Dion and Bouton had turned to the development of the car, and the torch they had lit was taken up by two young Russian émigrés resident in Paris, the brothers Michel and Eugene Werner. In 1896, they had fitted a De Dion Bouton-type engine to a bicycle frame, at first at the rear, but later over the front wheel.

Though prone to side-slip, the front-wheel-drive Werner achieved considerable popularity. However, better things were on the way, and the 1901 'new position' Werner, with the engine housed within a diamond frame, in roughly the same position as a cycle's pedalling mechanism, set a pattern which was to be followed to the present day.

It was around that time, too, that one of the greatest names in motorcycling began to be heard. This was Peugeot, today the oldest surviving company in the industry, whose vee-twins soon became much sought after. A Peugeot vee-twin engine, indeed, brought Norton victory in the first (1907) Isle of Man TT race; and by 1913 the same makers were already developing a very sophisticated overhead-camshaft vertical twin.

But the bulk of the French market was for ultra-lightweights, mostly pedal-assisted, and it is no surprise that France is still a major supplier of mopeds today.

The English member of the 1895 trio, Colonel Holden, had his factory (The British Motor Traction Company) at Kennington Oval. The four-cylinder Holden was, in its later form, claimed to have a maximum speed of 39 km/h (24 mph). Not that the gallant Colonel had much chance of showing off the model's paces. Britain's magisterial classes were still living in the age of the horse, and there was an overall limit of 6 km/h (4 mph) on the roads. Even then a mechanically propelled vehicle had to be accompanied by a man with a red flag. That law was repealed and the limit raised to 19 km/h (12 mph) in 1896. The London-to-Brighton Veteran Car Run is an annual thanksgiving for this emancipation.

Unhampered by such restrictions, the Continentals gaily began racing from one city to another. It was largely because competition led to technical improvement in France and Belgium that these nations emerged as leaders of the new mechanical revolution. When Britain's motorcycle industry began to get under way, around the turn of the century, the engines fitted were, in the main, imported units of De Dion, Minerva, Aster, Kalecom, or other Continental makes. Nor was that all. Riding on the back of the booming cycle industry of Coventry, some rather sharp financiers were out to feather

their own nests by buying up whatever British rights to Continental patents happened to be lying about. One such buyer was Harry J. Lawson, who had been instrumental in forming the Humber Company, among others. Late in 1895, Lawson acquired a parcel of Daimler and De Dion patents and set up the British Motor Syndicate and, a year later, produced a British copy of the De Dion tricycle, though with one essential difference: this time the engine was ahead of the rear axle and, in consequence, the machine was far more manageable. A year or so later, the name changed to the Motor Manufacturing Company. The company produced copies of the Werner motorcycle, and supplied Coventry-built copies of the De Dion engine to bicycle makers such as Excelsior, who were now entering the motorcycle field.

By the early 1900s the motorcycle was well on its way, but one trouble was that nobody knew quite where the engine should go. In Paris, the Werners were producing a model in which the engine was mounted ahead of the steering column, and drove the front wheel by a round-section, twisted-rawhide belt. Raleigh, in Britain, had a somewhat similar design. Royal Enfield mounted the engine in the same position, but took the drive to the rear wheel by a very long, crossed belt. Both Beeston and Ormonde mounted the engine to the rear of the pedalling-gear bottom bracket, roughly where the gearbox would be located in later years. Singer bought up the ingenious Perks and Birch arrangement of a small engine housed within a cast-aluminium spoked wheel. Humber came to an arrangement with Phelon and Moore whereby it employed the engine as a structural part of the frame, replacing the front-down tube. However, the majority of the smaller companies merely clipped an engine (usually a Minerva) to the front of the front-down tube of a conventional bicycle.

The drawback to the high-built bicycle, with high-mounted engine, was that it had a shocking tendency to lie down at the slightest hint of mud, and because tarred roads were few and far between at this time, there was mud in abundance on country road and city street alike. The Werner brothers hit on the logical position for the engine when, in 1902, they abandoned the earlier mounting ahead of the steering column and, instead, put it within the frame, where the bottom bracket of the pedalling mechanism had been. With the very much lower centre of gravity thus obtained, the motorcycle became safer and far more easy to handle.

Not until 1903, when John A. Prestwich, of London, produced a 293 cc single-cylinder side-valve engine for general sale, did a British-built proprietary engine become available. Later the same year, White and Peppe, of Coventry, entered the field with a 500 cc side-valve in which the inlet and exhaust valves were very widely

Far left: It is doubtful that this 1904 Humber was so well burnished on the day that it first left the Coventry, England factory where it was born.

Left: Superbike of a bygone age. This giant sportster built by Motosacoche in Switzerland has a vee-twin engine of 1,000 cc.

Below: This finely-restored 3½ hp Chater-Lea was produced near London in 1905 – just five years after the firm was founded.

Previous pages: As far back as 1919, this American Indian had leaf-springing on front and rear wheels.

Left: Vintage machines still take part in competitions. This racing Velocette is being ridden by ex-road-race star Bill Lomas.

Above: Built in Copenhagen, this four-cylinder Nimbus has shaft drive and a telescopic front fork.

Right: The Zenith Gradua with its variable gearing operated by the handle above the tank.

separated; it was a design of extraordinary longevity, because it was to be the mainstay of the Aeriel motorcycle right up to 1925.

The first generation of motorcycle engines had but one mechanically operated valve, and that was the exhaust; the inlet valve was provided with a light spring, and was sucked open to admit fresh gas by the downward movement of the piston within the cylinder. Nor was the fresh gas produced by a jet or spray carburettor at first. Instead, part of the sheet-tin fuel tank was fabricated to form a shallow tray. Sometimes the exhaust pipe was diverted to pass through this compartment to assist in vaporization, but usually an engine had to struggle along as best it might, by scooping up petrol gas produced by the jiggling about of the shallow layer of petrol in the tray. The apparatus was known, rather grandly, as the surface carburettor. Ignition systems were crude and generally coil-and-battery of a sort. Again, 1903 is the significant date, for in that year the Bosch company of Germany, introduced the first practical high-tension magneto.

Unreliability was the bugbear of the early motorcycle, for metallurgy was yet in its infancy, and engineers proceeded by trial and error rather than by the book. It was by no means uncommon for a valve to function more and more weakly, and finally fail to open at all, as its operating cam reverted to a circular form. Flimsy accumulators lived in cupboards in the petrol tank, where they danced about until they fell to pieces. Round or flat driving belts broke with depressing frequency, and not until the leather or rubber-and-canvas vee belt was adopted, around 1902, did any relatively satisfactory form of transmission emerge.

There was a reason for a rider's preference for belt drive. No shock absorber was fitted to the engine shaft or rear hub, and the 'give' of a belt ironed out the fluctuations that would be transmitted by a roller chain or spur gearing. The Singer motor wheel, which had spur gearing at first, made a noise like a demented threshing machine as road grit contributed to rapid wear of the cogs. This problem was overcome in later models by dispensing with direct drive and, instead, using chain drive by way of a countershaft in the bottom-bracket position. Little wonder, therefore, that the motorcyclist of the early

1900s had to be not only dedicated but an instinctive trouble-shooter. Should his machine break down on a run he could not rely on help being at hand. Garages, such as existed, were apt to be ignorant of mechanical matters.

It was the Triumph company that brought respectability to motor-cycledom. Not that its machines were outstandingly new in design. On the contrary, Triumph was content to lag behind slightly in adopting novelty – but the models were made of better quality materials and put together more carefully than those of many of Triumph's competitors. In World War I – and that was now not so very far ahead – dispatch-riders gave the Triumph the nickname of 'Trusty', and that was to remain the telegraphic address of the factory for the next several decades.

While speeds were low, lack of any form of springing at front or rear was of minor consequence. But as engines began to gain power, so frame breakages became more common. Additional struts to the front fork blades proved not to be the answer, and, gradually, front springing became essential. Some factories devised their own systems. In Britain, Triumph evolved a fork, pivoting at the base of the steering head and moving fore-and-aft under the control of a single horizontal spring. Rex opted for a clumsy arrangement of twin-tube fork blades, incorporating spring-controlled sliders. From France came the Truffault, a pivoted type of fork which predated the generally similar Earles fork by almost 50 years. The rest of the motorcycle industry waited for a saviour – who came along in 1906. Alfred Drew was his name, and his invention was the parallel-ruler fork with a compression spring at each side.

For the early, low-power, motorcycle engine, hills posed a problem, and the first solution on offer was the variable-gear pulley. The idea was that by closing the sides of the engine pulley the groove would be narrowed and the belt would operate at a greater radius, so raising the overall ratio; alternatively, opening the pulley sides would lower the ratio. Gear changing in this fashion could not be done on the move. Instead, on reaching the foot of a hill, the rider had to dismount, remove the driving belt, adjust the driving pulley to suit, then refit the belt, probably after shortening it by removing a link or two. After he surmounted the hill, he had to go through the entire procedure again to get back into high gear.

But two British factories thought up a refinement of this scheme. They were Zenith and Rudge-Whitworth, who evolved the Zenith Gradua and Rudge Multi variable gears, respectively. In each case, the opening or closing of the pulleys was done on the move. The Zenith plot, operated by a 'coffee-grinder' handle above the petrol tank and involving an arrangement obevel gears and chains, moved the rear wheel backward or forward in the fork to keep the tension of the driving belt constant. So effective was the Zenith Gradua system that machines so equipped began to gather hill-climbing trophies by the hatful – until the governing body of the sport stepped in to ban the Zenith from entering such competitions. Gleefully, Fred Barnes, the boss of Zenith, sketched a new trade mark in which the Zenith name was part hidden by a superimposed grid and the slogan 'Barred'. It was the best possible publicity for the make.

The catalyst for a proper countershaft gear-box was the decision to switch the Tourist Trophy races for 1911 to the Isle of Man Mountain Circuit. This meant a sustained climb from near sea level at Ramsey, to around 300 m (1,000 ft) on the flanks of Snaefell. Significantly, the first three places in the Senior race were taken by American-made Indian vee-twins, equipped with all-chain drive, two-speed, countershaft gear-boxes, and plate clutches. Before long, transmissions of this kind were being seen on standard roadster models.

Isolated by the wide Atlantic from the mainstream of motorcycle development, it is understandable that the native American powered two-wheeler should evolve along individual lines. Though it is customary to think of the typical transatlantic model as a massive, if woolly vee-twin, in fact the early machines were single-cylinder models, as elsewhere.

However, the American fashion was to slope the engine rearward and incorporate it as the saddle member of the frame. Such was the first Indian, built by Oscar Hedstrom as far back as 1901. Power output was no more than $1\frac{3}{4}$ hp, but the machine was an instant success, and in 1902 Hedstrom and his partner, George Hendee, built and sold 143 of them.

What was to become the Indian's biggest rival, the Harley-Davidson, began in a backyard shed in 1903 when William Harley and Arthur Davidson put together a light 2 hp single. Six years later the vee-twin

Far top left : The name that appeared on the world's fastest production machine of the 1950s.

Far centre left : Plated tanks were a feature of Coventry-built Montgomerys of the 1930s.

Far bottom left : A really rare machine. Zedel provided engines from 1902 to many Continental manufacturers.

Top : The actual Brough Superior that held the Brooklands lap record before the circuit closed at the outbreak of the second World War.

Above : Famous name, famous insignia. Scott-built two-stroke twins that are much sought after today.

Left : Once a great name in the French industry, Terrot is now part of the Peugeot empire.

was introduced, and the archetypal USA motorcycle had taken shape.

They were by no means the only makers, and Flying Merkel, Emblem, Thor, Pope, Iver-Johnson, and Excelsior could each claim their band of faithful followers. All made vee-twins, for the small-capacity two-stroke lightweight – with one exception – failed to gain much recognition in America. That exception was the little Cleveland, introduced in 1914, which was still in production 12 years later, not only for home consumption but for world-wide markets as well.

There was one other type, however, which the USA made very much its own, and that was the in-line four. Among the earliest builders of the type was Pierce-Arrow. The Pierce-Arrow bike was a light and handy model of which the frame top tube served as the fuel tank. William Henderson however, brought the type to perfection, from the introduction of the first machine to carry his name in 1911.

Production of the Henderson was taken over, a few years later, by the Chicago-based Excelsior company, but Henderson himself soon left to start again – with another four-in-line, the Ace. In turn, the Ace was absorbed into the Indian range after Henderson had been killed in a road accident.

One other four-in-line is worth mentioning because it was the rather unexpected product of Cleveland, the company which had built its reputation on small two-strokes. Again, there was Henderson influence, because its designer, Everitt de Long, had trained at both the Henderson and Ace works.

Sadly, the comparatively cheap Detroit-built, mass-produced car killed off the American motorcycle until, in the final stages, just Indian and Harley-Davidson remained. Now, there's Harley alone.

Another facet of motorcycling had been cut, with the introduction of the lightweight utility machine, powered by a small two-stroke engine. The two-stroke principle had been around for quite a while, though it didn't come into general use for small motorcycles until about 1911. The biggest fillip to the lightweight movement in Britain came with the announcement of a proprietary 269 cc engine – to be sold complete with magneto and exhaust system – by Villiers of Wolverhampton. Villiers had earlier been producing a lightweight inlet-over-exhaust four-stroke engine, but this didn't get anything like the reception from the trade that the two-stroke unit received. Now, with a suitably cheap proprietary engine, a set of front forks from Druid or Saxon, frame lugs from Brampton or BSA and a gearbox from Sturmey-Archer, any small firm could become a motorcycle manufacturer – and many did. There would have been even more save that war had come in 1914, and the motorcycle industry was channelled toward the war effort.

The period after the war is known as the 'Golden Age' of motor-cycles. At the start, the machine still had a rigid frame, flat tank, acetylene gas lighting, exposed valves and, in many cases, belt drive and hand-operated, total-loss lubrication. At the end, the motorcycle was pretty much as we know it now. Saddle tank, electric lighting, chain drive, even positive-stop, foot-operated gear changing had been invented. To some extent, Continental design was the prime mover of innovations. As early as 1920, Carlo Guzzi had built a horizontal single with shaft-and-bevel drive to an overhead camshaft, hairpin valve springs, and a three-speed gear-box in unit with the engine. By 1923, BMW had a transverse flat-twin with shaft final drive, while Bianchi, in Italy, was producing a beautiful little double-overhead-camshaft engine with total enclosure of the valve mechanism.

'Racing,' said the pundits, 'improves the breed'. And so it did, because racing practice sparked off many of the improvements seen on roadster motorcycles – better quality valve steels, light-alloy pistons, and wired-on tyres. In fact, wired-on tyres fiad been employed as early as 1912 on the 'TT Model' BSA, and it is surprising that they were not brought into general use until the middle to late 1920s. The positive-stop gear change, now in world-wide use, was the brain-wave of Harold Willis, race-shop chief at the Velocette works, who got the idea from observing the mechanism of a metal-shaping machine.

Not all the developments met with lasting success, although they were popular for a while. One such was the double-diameter-piston Dunelt two-stroke, built in Birmingham by an offshoot of a still very active steel company. This engine ran on the conventional two-stroke principle of drawing the petrol gas into the crankcase, where it was compressed before being shot up the transfer passage into the combustion chamber; so far, so good, but Dunelt's scheme was to use a stepped piston, larger in diameter at the base than at the crown, so that the compression of the gas in the crankcase would be increased.

Forerunner of the popular 'Boy Racer' 7R AJS, this 1937 example, now lovingly restored, has a chain-driven overhead camshaft and girder front forks. Throughout its 60-year history, the company produced dozens of different racing machines.

'Semi-supercharged,' said Dunelt in its advertising. It worked, too, but even the makers had lost faith in the idea by 1930, and reverted to a conventional two-stroke engine.

Vitesse, who supplied two-stroke engines to the Sun company, came up with the idea of a rotary disc in the crankcase, to increase volumetric efficiency. Again, the idea was fine – indeed, exactly the same plot is used today in certain road-racing engines – but, alas for Vitesse, the metals of the day were not quite up to the job and, after perservering for a couple of years, Sun abandoned the scheme.

Up in Glasgow, Barr and Stroud had made its name in the manufacture of precision gun equipment for the Royal Navy. But for a few years in the early 1920s it launched into proprietary engine manufacture with a sleeve-valve unit (350 and 500 cc singles, plus a 1,000 cc vee-twin), on the Burt-McCallum system. This was beautifully silent in operation, emitting little more than a silky rustle. In fact, a Barr and Stroud engine was the heart of the Packman and Peppe 'Silent Three', and worked well enough so long as only a modest power output was demanded. But the sleeve was driven by an integral knob on the hem of its skirt and because the component lacked suitable metal, the knob tended to break away. So the Barr and Stroud was discontinued, but the design was indeed a sound one, for it was later to form the basis of the famous Bristol Hercules sleeve-valve aero engine.

Yet another out-of-the-rut engine was the Bradshaw, which employed a wet liner sunk deeply into a smooth-surfaced crankcase. A rotary pump picked up oil from the sump and sluiced it around

the outside of the wet liner for cooling purposes, the same oil serving also to lubricate the unit. For a while the Bradshaw engine more than held its own in the competitions field, but it was a comparatively expensive engine to build, and it was given what proved to be a death-blow by the Triumph company's introduction, in 1925, of the 494 cc Model P.

Lighting at first had been almost universally by acetylene gas. Water was allowed to drip on to calcium carbide to serve as a miniature portable gasworks, carried on the machine. A refinement, though not brought into universal service, was the use of compressed acetylene gas, obtainable in exchange bottles. However, electric lighting crept onto the scene from 1919 onwards. Here the Americans led the way, although dynamo lighting was offered on Granville Bradshaw's 1919 ABC twin. Acceptance came with the development of the Lucas Magdyno, a compact unit in which a direct-current dynamo was mounted above and driven from, a magneto. A cheaper, alternative system came from the Morris-Lister company – this was the ML Maglita, in which dynamo and magneto windings were carried on a single armature. But the drawback was that, in order to generate enough lighting current, the instrument had to run at engine speed – and that meant that the sparking plug fired every time the piston came to the top of the stroke. The idle spark mattered little provided the engine was properly timed, but should it occur when the inlet valve was open – whoosh! Send for the fire brigade!

Carburetion too, underwent a process of steady development as the spray or jet carburettor took over. An early example was the Leaguemare, built in France.

By the mid 1930s, some designers were turning their attention to keeping the rider clean. New Hudson, for example, produced a series of models in which the lower part of the engine, and the gear-box,

were shrouded behind detachable pressed-steel bonnets (the idea was copied by Triumph too). From Coventry-Eagle, a firm which had advanced the cause of the pressed-steel frame, came the luxurious Pullman, with leaf-sprung rear wheel. But the most successful design of them all was the Francis-Barnett Cruiser.

Immediately after the end of World War I, a number of factories had rushed out rear-sprung machines. Matchless had the Model H, with quite a modern-looking swinging-arm frame. Coulson-Black-burne used leaf springs and a bell-crank arrangement – and demonstrated the effectiveness of the system by engaging a well-known racing man to ride one without a rear tyre. The trouble with springing systems of this kind was that the only damping available was by friction, and general acceptance of rear springing had to await the coming of the hydraulically-damped spring unit, in the late 1940s.

Pioneered on road-racing machines (first BMW, then Norton) the telescopic front fork was further developed during World War II by the Matchless factory, on the 350 cc G3L Model used by thousands of British Army dispatch riders. The Matchless Teledraulic fork combined spring suspension with oil damping, and this formula was to become standard practice in the years ahead. Wartime, too, had seen the beginnings of the alternator as a replacement for the dynamo in the generation of electric current, when the first simple example was specified for the 350 cc twin which Triumph was to build for army service. Unfortunately, the Coventry blitz put paid to that scheme, and so the alternator had to await the return of peace before it became a commonplace part of a motorcycle's specification.

The story has come more-or-less up to date, with the motorcycle in its present state of development. The future could be a different tale, with turbines, or rotary-piston motors, but that is a matter for the technicians – and the crystal gazers.

GREAT NAMES

Throughout the history of
the motorcycle, men with dreams
have founded factories.
Many companies floundered along
the way, but some survived,
their products keeping pace with
the changing demands of
a fickle public. Yet even those
companies that went to the
wall wrote some part in the story
of the motorcycle.

No-one could now accurately state just how many motorcycle firms have been founded since the industry began, but intelligent estimates put the number at certainly no less than a staggering 2,000 spread among nearly 30 countries of the world.

Britain has been by far the most prolific of all producers, with something like 570 manufacturers, followed by Germany with around 200 less, and then Italy and France, whose scores stand at about 250 each.

Records of most of these great pioneers now remain only in history books, and most of their products have rusted away or been rendered down to scrap decades ago. But some models still survive in the dedicated hands of enthusiasts.

In the same way, some manufacturers had but brief glory before some disaster caused their demise – while others went on, surviving depressions and wars until they became truly famous, not just to the motorcycle world, but as household words known to all.

NORTON

James Lansdowne Norton showed promise as an engineer even as a lad, when his model steam engines attracted crowds in his home town. His apprenticeship to a tool maker was to prove useful, when he started the Norton Manufacturing Company in the late 19th century. Before long he switched from making bicycle components to constructing motorcycles, marketing his first Clement-powered model in 1902.

James's business skills did not match up to his engineering talents, unfortunately, and the new company was in trouble until he merged with one of his suppliers, R. T. Shelley, to form Norton Motors Ltd. The partnership was a huge success, and left 'Pa' Norton time to concentrate on development work. It was his tuning that helped Rem Fowler pilot a 617 cc vee-twin Peugeot-powered Norton to victory in the first-ever TT in 1907.

By 1909 only two of the range used proprietary engines, both 2½ hp JAPs. The other six used Norton's own engines, ranging from 3½ to 5 hp. Norton could certainly pick the right dealers for these new models – his two London agents were Harrods and Gamage's. Their faith in Norton was justified, for before 1914 the 490 cc sv Norton broke 112 British and world records, regularly exceeding 130 km/h (80 mph). During the war Norton supplied machines to the Russian Army, and moved to the renowned Bracebridge Street works.

Norton's post-war range included the three-speed, all-chain-drive, 633 cc, single-cylinder 'Big Four', which was to become one of his most successful models for everyday solo and sidecar use. Following the common practice of basing road-going models on sporting successes, the range also included the super-sport 'BS' model – guaranteed to exceed 120 km/h (75 mph). During the next few years, Norton's began to establish a sporting reputation that was to last for the next half-century.

A second place in the first post-war Senior TT by Dougie Brown in the three-speed sv model was not good enough for Pa Norton. In 1922 Norton achieved 158 km/h (98 mph) with the first outing of the new 490 cc ohv model, and the Model 18 – with its new, internally expanding drum brakes – was soon accepted as the fastest standard single of its day. In the 1923 TT the new model gained second place in the Senior, while an overbored 600 cc version came second in the new sidecar class.

To remind the public of Norton's road-going potential, Norton took a machine assembled from parts picked at random by the Auto Cycle Union (ACU) and proceeded to break 18 world records with it at Brooklands. In recognition of this the ACU awarded the company the newly established Maudes Trophy. Norton took the Trophy again the following year with an ACU-observed run from Land's End to John O' Groats – four times. To make the year complete, Alec Bennett rode his Norton to a Senior TT victory.

James Norton died the next year (1925), having seen Norton motorcycles well on the way to world-wide recognition. That same year Norton's won road-racing championships in Switzerland, Russia, Poland, Italy, Holland, Denmark and Hungary. Other Norton victories included the Ulster and Belgian *Grands Prix*, and of course the TT, as well as a third Maudes Trophy.

The 1926 TT saw the first outing for Norton's new works rider – Stanley Woods. Needless to say, he won the Senior. In traditional Norton fashion, the four-speed gearbox and dry-sump lubrication system used on his TT model were offered to the public at the 1926 Show, and the booming sales that resulted enabled Norton to invest some of the profits in developing new models – such as the overhead cam machine on which Alec Bennett won the 1927 Senior TT.

The next year the new 'Cammy' Norton was offered to the public. The ohv ES2, equipped with saddle tank and a new frame, was also introduced. In the meantime, Bert Denley had ridden his 500 cc ohv model into history by covering more than 160 km (100 miles) in an hour, and showed his versatility by winning several major trials as well.

During the next 10 years Norton continued to develop roadsters. Oil-bath primary chaincases became a standard feature, as did three-spring girder forks, while four-speed Norton gearboxes replaced the earlier three-speed Sturmey-Archer units. In racing the company continued its incredible record of successes at home and abroad, including gaining first, second and third places in the 1933 Senior TT.

During World War II, Norton's produced 16H sv 500 cc models and 600 cc ohv Big Fours for the Army, many fitted with sidecars.

Previous pages: The most popular racing machine ever produced, the Manx Norton put up an incredible series of Isle of Man TT performances. A detuned version, the International was made for fast road work. Men who rode to fame on the Manx include Geoff Duke and John Surtees.

Left: Still active at Vintage Club race meetings, the single-overhead-camshaft Norton of the 1930s is more than a match for many other much later sportsters.

Below: Norton were late onto the market with an electric starter. But, when it came, it really updated the old Commando design to this 850 cc sports model, which also features a rubber-mounted engine to cut down the effects of engine vibration.

In 1946 the 16H was retained, and was joined by the ohv model 18. Within a year, telescopic forks and plunger rear suspension were introduced.

Norton continued to dominate the racing scene, with the new breed of Cammy Nortons, known as the International, and the classic Manx Norton. In 1949 the Model 7 500 cc ohv twin appeared, soon called the Dominator. It was enlarged through the years to 600, then 650 cc, and is the ancestor of the modern 850 cc Commando.

In the late '50s, foreign competition from firms such as Gilera and MV at last robbed Norton of world-wide dominance in road racing. The road models, possibly because of their sporting background, continued to sell and by 1963 the range included the 250 cc twin Jubilee (introduced in 1958), 500 and 650 cc Dominators with the race-proved 'Featherbed' frames and 'Roadholder' forks, the 350 cc ohv Model 50 and the 500 cc ES2. By now Norton was part of the AMC group, but after many changes of name the company has survived under the Norton Villiers Triumph banner, and still produces the 850 cc Commando and the Easyrider moped.

HARLEY-DAVIDSON

Last of the big-time American manufacturers born during the very early days of the industry is Harley-Davidson, founded by William S. Harley and Arthur Davidson back in 1903. From the very start, the firm specialized in big-capacity machines producing single cylinder and vee-twin engines built into their own frames.

Pre-World-War I production featured 350 cc and 500 cc singles and twin-cylinder machines of between 750 cc and 1,200 cc.

It was not until the late 1950s that Harley-Davidson moved into the small-bike field, but when they made the change they did it in a big way. In 1959 the company, based at Milwaukee, began production of their own scooter, but the biggest change came a year later with a merger with the Italian Aer-Macchi concern. The joining of the two famous names – Aer-Macchi had a long and glorious history of motorcycle and aircraft manufacturing – produced an even larger range, starting with under-200 cc two-strokes right up to the mighty over-1,000 cc vee-twins.

Besides the Italian-styled lightweights, Harleys have made one major concession to foreign competition. Besides the huge 1,200 cc Electra Glide, they now offer stripped-down models. The 1,000 cc Sportster has a fairly long history, but the 1,200 cc FX with its Sportster styling and bigger engine is seemingly designed to compete with lighter, faster competitors. Nevertheless, all the big twins remain uniquely Harley-Davidson in their styling.

Although their offerings remain the biggest crowd pullers and occupy a unique niche in motorcycling folk lore, Harleys have taken a great interest in sport recently, particularly to promote the lightweights. They have won the 250 cc World Championship for the last three years, and also took the 350 cc class in 1976. The big twins still dominate dirt racing in the United States, and have taken their share of world records.

Right: Harley-Davidson machines may be heavy and very expensive outside America but, for long-distance freeway cruising, the big vee-twins are in a class of their own.

Below: Flash-back to 1914. The engine layout was, even then, two cylinders in vee formation. And effortless, high-speed work for mile after mile was the idea behind the design.

TRIUMPH

Siegfried Bettman, a 21-year-old German immigrant, had been in England for only a year when, bored by a series of dead-end jobs, he decided to set up in business for himself and launched an import-export agency. He specialized in exporting bicycles made by Williams Andrews of Birmingham and marketed under his own name. Realizing that the bikes would sell better with a catchier title, Bettman sought one that would be understandable in English, German or French. The name he chose was Triumph. In 1887 he took on a partner, a young German engineer called Mauritz Schulte. Deciding that their future lay in the manufacture of their own cycles, the pair moved from London to Coventry, centre of the bicycle industry, where they started producing machines in 1889. By the turn of the century the Triumph Cycle Company (thanks to substantial investment by Dunlop Tyres) was flourishing. In the last few years of the 19th century the partners had experimented with various engines, and in 1902 announced the first Triumph motorcycle, powered by a 239 cc Minerva engine. Within three years they were using their own 3 hp engine.

The year 1907 was particularly important for Triumph. For the first time annual sales exceeded 1,000 bikes, and Jack Marshall won the first-ever TT on a 3½ hp single-cylinder Triumph. More racing successes followed, helping the company to sell over 3,000 machines in 1909. Some of the profits went into developing the 500 cc Model H which was announced in 1914. Over 30,000 of these were to be supplied to the Allied armies during the next four years, helping Triumph to enter peacetime on a secure footing. New models developed during the war soon made their appearance.

Possibly Triumph's most interesting model to date, the 'Ricci' made its debut in 1921. Developed by Harry Ricardo and named after him, this 500 cc four-valve single developed about 20 bhp. Before it was dropped in 1928, the Ricardo was to establish for Triumph a sporting image that has stuck. Several advanced features incorporated in the model, such as its dry-sump lubrication system, were to help with Triumph's development for the next 40 years. A new designer, Val Page, joined the company in 1932, and within a year he had developed a 650 cc vertical twin that won Triumph its first Maudes Trophy by covering 800 kilometres (500 miles) in as many minutes. It also set the pattern for future models, for it was five years later that the Edward Turner-designed 500 cc vertical twin was announced. It was called the Speed Twin, and was to be the first of a whole new breed.

With the outbreak of World War II, Triumph, in common with other leading manufacturers, developed prototypes for military use. Norton, BSA, Matchless and the rest offered a variety of 350 cc and 500 cc big singles. Triumph, using the benefit of pre-war twin experience, offered two vertical twins. The 350 cc ohv 3TW was unique in that it was the first production machine to be equipped with alternator lighting, while the 500 cc sv 5TW set another precedent with telescopic rather than girder forks. Neither model was as successful as the single-cylinder competitors, but both served as useful test beds for peace-time models. In fact a 5TW, in civilian TRW guise and ridden by Bill Randall, went on to win a gold medal in the 1949 ISDT.

With the success of Triumph's vertical twins, it was inevitable that other manufacturers would follow suit. BSA produced its 'A' series, and Norton quickly followed with the Dominator 88 and 99. Triumph retaliated with the TR5 Trophy, and the 650 cc 6T Thunderbird, and with the exception of the 150 cc Terrier and the 200 cc Tiger Cub, the entire post-war production was geared to the two-cylinder design.

Triumph was absorbed by the huge BSA Group in 1951, but machines were still developed and sold independently under the Triumph banner. A notable example was a sporty 650 cc model, first introduced in 1959 and named the Bonneville. Only two years later the name was proven apt when Bill Johnson screamed across the Bonneville Salt Flats in a twin-engined streamliner to establish a new world record at 361.41 km/h (224.57 mph) – a speed that was to stand until 1975.

By the late 1960s, despite the introduction of the unit-construction Bonneville, Triumph needed something with which to compete effectively with the new crop of Japanese and European 'Superbikes'. The Doug Hele-designed Trident was offered, in 1968, as the answer. It broke with tradition in that it was a 750 cc ohv triple, and immediately achieved great success both on the road and on the track. Between 1971 and 1976 a Trident, nicknamed 'Slippery Sam' won the Production TT every year, and in 1972 a factory Trident also won the TT Formula 750 class. While Triumph bikes were still selling well, however, the BSA-Triumph group as a whole was in serious financial difficulties. In fact a projected 350 cc ohc twin Triumph Fury was dropped in 1971 for lack of funds. With government aid, a new parent company was formed under the name Norton Villiers Triumph. Despite more government investment, the group has not flourished. In 1975 the government backed the forming of the worker-controlled Meriden Co-operative, which continued making 750 cc twins.

Right: With an advanced specification of three cylinders and an electric starter, the 750 cc Triumph Trident is a favourite of the British bike enthusiast. Sports models of the same design were unbeatable in Isle of Man production-machine races.

Below: The 650 cc Triumph Thunderbird – built in 1950, when Britain led the world in motorcycle engineering, styling and design. The general engine format lives on today in the current 750 cc twins built at Meriden.

HONDA

At the end of World War II Japan was in a state of chaos. Public transport was almost non-existent, and the demand for a cheap form of utility transport was immense. This was the situation in 1946 when Soichiro Honda, a 40-year-old engineer, came across an army surplus consignment of 500 two-stroke stationary engines. He bought them cheaply, and later that year set up a small, primitive factory with only 12 workers to modify the engines to fit bicycles. Produced at only one a day, and fuelled by spirit distilled from pine trees, they were nevertheless much in demand. By 1949, Honda Motorcycles was producing complete machines. Using a two-stroke single, the machine was named the Dream and was to mark the start of the most successful motorcycle company the world has ever seen.

Before long the company was selling over 250 machines a week and, despite money problems, brought out the E-type Dream in 1951. This set a precedent, for it was powered by a four-stroke engine, as were all Hondas for the next 20 years. The Cub, a step-through-styled utility model, was announced in 1952, and so successful was it that the Emperor of Japan awarded Honda the Blue Ribbon Medal for services to Japan. A huge programme of re-tooling resulted in a production line capable of producing 1,000 of the new Benley 90 cc singles every month by 1953. But the new company found itself in some difficulties at this point, partly financial, as all the new equipment was expensive. Also, while Honda was the first Japanese manufacturer to open up after the war, by the mid '50s there were more than 70 competitors, all after the same market. Nevertheless, with nearly three-quarters of the home market in its grasp, Honda was still in a strong position. The company survived, and Mr Honda turned his attention to two new fields – exports and racing.

In 1954 he visited the TT as an observer, and four years later the first Hondas were sold in England, Holland and America. That same year, 1958, Honda launched the 50 cc C100, selling well over 20,000 within a year. From this point the company went from strength to strength. In 1960, after an unsuccessful attempt the previous year, a Honda 250 cc came fourth in the TT, and Honda started to contest *Grands Prix* all over Europe. The next year, only two years after entering races, Hondas won the 125 cc and 250 cc World Championship classes. This incredible success was reflected in sales.

An American subsidiary had been started in 1959. Now a West German company was set up to look after European sales. Honda was able to devote more energy to the development of racing machines. Bikes were raced in the 50 cc, 125 cc, 250 cc and 350 cc classes. Again the successes were staggering. Against all European competition, Hondas took the 125 cc, 250 cc and 350 cc world titles. The success spiral continued as racing victories promoted higher sales, which in turn financed the development of better racing machines.

Exports in 1962 rose to 114,000 bikes, while total production passed 1,000,000. Next year's figures speak for themselves. 1963 exports were 338,000 machines. Annual production was 1,250,000. Honda had become what it is today – the biggest motorcycle manufacturing company in the world.

Honda now started moving in on the British and American markets in a big way. The first Hondas reached dealers in the summer of 1960. The Benley 125 cc ohc twin was offered as a standard C92, a sports CS92 and a super-sports CB92. Its stable-mate, the 259 cc ohc twin Dream came in a standard C71 version, which was soon superseded by the C72, featuring wet-sump lubrication and 12 volt lighting, while the CS72 catered for riders wanting a sporty version. In 1964, having gained publicity by taking the Maudes Trophy the previous year, Hondas won the 125 cc and 350 cc World Championship classes and

Above: Honda and Hailwood, the combination of man and machine that became a road-racing legend. Determined to break into world markets in a big way, Honda built a series'of exotic racers and hired the great Mike Hailwood to win on them.

lapped the TT course at more than 160 km/h (100 mph).

Three years later Honda retired from *Grand Prix* racing. The 250 cc and 297 cc six-cylinder racers were made useless when the *FIM* imposed a four-cylinder limit on racing machines – and while the company could doubtless have developed competitive machines to the new standards, it didn't need to. Honda had entered racing primarily to publicize and sell road bikes. Honda was now well established as a top-selling manufacturer, and underlined this with the millionth Honda motorcycle to be purchased in the USA. That same year the 10-millionth Honda rolled off the production lines. Honda had shown the world that whatever any other manufacturer could do, it could, and would, do better.

Up to 1969 Honda had concentrated on small- and medium-capacity bikes. In that year Honda branched out into the big-bike market. Most of the sales had been in the 50 cc to 250 cc bracket, while the biggest model had been the 450 cc twin model nicknamed the 'Black Bomber'. Now the company unveiled the CB750 four-cylinder ohc model, and soon followed it up with a 500 cc version. Honda entered a 750 in the Classic Daytona 200, and won, to gain publicity for the new model. The firm also went on to win the 24-hour Bol d'Or at Le Mans and followed that up by winning the 500 cc Production TT the following year.

Now the Honda range stretches from 50 cc mopeds to the mighty 1,000 cc, flat-four, water-cooled Gold Wing. Honda makes bikes for trials, moto-cross and road racing – and has re-entered racing with a new range of machines. In 1975 Honda roadsters proved themselves by taking the first six places in the 500 cc Production TT.

BSA

Many British motorcycle manufacturers can trace their histories back to the late 19th century – a few were started even earlier. But BSA predates them all with ease, for the company's roots can be traced back as far as 1689! The reason is that 'BSA' stands for Birmingham Small Arms, and it was in 1689 that William II, desperate for guns to defend England against attacks from France, contracted to buy his guns from the many excellent gunsmiths in Birmingham. For the next 150 years the Birmingham gunsmiths supplied arms for the British Army, until in 1861 their Trade Association formed a public company: the Birmingham Small Arms Company Limited. The company's fortunes were mixed. At one point, in 1878, it shut down completely for lack of work. The government then placed an order for more rifles, which kept some jobs going while the management looked around for new and profitable products.

Manufacture began in 1880 on E. F. C. Otto's new bicycle, and, a year later, BSA-designed bicycles – basically penny-farthings – also began to appear. Before long the company introduced the first 'safety' bicycle, with a chain-driven rear wheel. The factory was still heavily committed to gun manufacture, but by the turn of the century BSA was firmly established as a manufacturer of cycles and components. The first all-BSA cycle appeared in 1908, and a year later BSA

Above: With their four-cylinder Gold Wing introduced in the mid 1970s, Honda entered the luxury tourer market. This water-cooled multi-cylinder machine featured various exotic fitments, such as shaft final drive.

Below: Built with sidecar use in mind, this vee-twin BSA had a 500 cc overhead-valve engine. Produced in 1935, the machine still had exposed valve springs and, to prevent a rider's coat being sucked into the inlet tract, a guard was fitted over the mouth of the carburetter.

introduced its first motorcycle. Because of government contacts through its gun-making activities, BSA was well placed to win contracts for the supply of other military equipment when World War I broke out. During hostilities the company expanded to employ over 20,000 workers, and was in an exceptionally good economic position by 1918, when the company's cycle and motorcycle manufacturing divisions were formed into BSA Cycles Ltd. No longer were its products considered merely the side lines of a gun manufacturer.

During the slump of the early '20s, nearly half the BSA work force was laid off as some of BSA's subsidiaries collapsed. The motorcycles continued to sell well, however. Partly due to the size of the company, BSA was able to offer a huge range, varying from diminutive 150 cc four-stroke singles to the impressive 1,000 cc sv vee-twin. This established itself as a trustworthy sidecar mount and (with the sidecars custom built) was used as everything from taxi cab to butcher's delivery van. Two slogans dating from the '20s nicely sum up BSA's success: 'One in four is a BSA' and 'The most complete range ever offered by one firm'.

In 1923 BSA started using mass-production methods for the first time, on the little 250 cc 'round tank'. Ever eager to gain publicity, the firm sponsored a quartet of BSA riders who rode up Mt Snowdon. Even more impressive, in 1926 two BSA outfits were ridden round the world, covering 32,000 kilometres (20,000 miles) through 24 countries in 18 months.

During World War II BSA was again in the thick of it, supplying scout cars, rifles, machine-guns, and, of course, motorcycles to the British forces. The firm was the largest supplier of motorcycles to the British Army, delivering no less than 126,344 between 1939 and 1945. Most were sv 500 cc M20s, which were slow, at around 80 km/h (50 mph), but earned a great reputation for reliability – a reputation that BSA was to put to good use after the war, as M20s and 600 cc M21s were sold right up to the early 60s. By the end of the war New Hudson, Sunbeam and Ariel Motor Cycles came under the BSA umbrella, and Triumph was acquired in 1951 – making BSA the largest motorcycle manufacturer in Western Europe.

By the mid '50s, despite disposing of some subsidiary companies, including BSA Cycles, the group had over 30 operating groups in almost as many factories. BSA motorcycles were being used by the AA, the RAC, the British Army and police forces all over the world. The 500 cc ohv twin A7 and its 750 'big brother' the A10 Golden Flash were among the most successful of the new breed of vertical twins, while the Gold Star ohv single, in 350 cc and 500 cc versions, was fast becoming accepted as a classic both by sportsmen and road-riding enthusiasts.

In 1967 the BSA group won the Queen's Award to Industry for its exports of BSAs and Triumphs – and won it again the next year when it accounted for 80 per cent of the British motorcycle industry's exports. Then in 1971, everything changed – the group made an enormous loss in one year. A bank loan was negotiated, and the 350 cc ohc twin Fury was introduced which, it was hoped, would boost sales – to no avail. The new model was dropped for lack of finance, redundancies and asset-selling started, and the government refused any further aid. The next year the group was incorporated into the new NVT Group, but BSA, as an independent company, was finished. BSA's last new model, the 750 cc triple Rocket Three was dropped from the range for the 1973 season.

Left: The 750 cc triple Rocket Three was the last new model to come out of an independent BSA. The model was dropped after BSA's merger with the NVT group.

Below: One of the most luxurious machines on the market, the 1,000 cc BMW is, for many, the ultimate for luxury high-speed touring. The machine, with its twin-cylinder engine, has shaft-drive to the rear wheel, eliminating the need for a chain.

BMW

In 1917 Germany was embroiled in the Great War. In an attempt to boost aircraft production, the Bayrische Motoren Werke was established to develop and construct aero engines. In 1919 an aircraft using an in-line six BMW engine was to set up a new world altitude record at 9,760 m (32,020 ft). There wasn't much demand for 22.9 litre aero engines in the post-war slump that gripped Germany in the early '20s, but there was a call for cheap transport. With this in mind, Max Fritz, a wartime aero-engine designer, set out to develop BMW's first motorcycle. Designated the R32, it was introduced at the Paris Show of 1923 and was an immediate success. The 496 cc sv engine was housed in a frame featuring leaf-spring front suspension and primitive disc brakes – revolutionary in the '20s. Two years later the 250 cc R11 appeared. Like the R32 it had shaft drive, but was a vertical single instead of a flat twin. The ohv engine developed 6.5 bhp, and helped consolidate BMW's growing reputation for quality. In 1928 a new range leader emerged: the 750 cc sv flat-twin R62. It was at this point that, in an attempt to gain publicity, BMW started on a series of world speed record attempts that was to establish it as a major contender in the world record stakes, and was also to help the development of design features that were to be successfully incorporated in later roadsters.

Between 1929 and 1932, Ernst Henne's efforts to stay ahead of English record contenders on 1,000 cc vee-twins paid handsomely. Henne drove his ohc 750 cc flat-twin BMW faster than any motor-cyclist had hitherto travelled. Henne pushed the record from 216.75 km/h (134.68 mph) up to 244.40 km/h (151.86 mph) in 1932. In the meantime the roadsters were not neglected. A 200 cc single was tried out in 1931 but proved unsuccessful. Sales of the other models were good, however, which helped BMW develop faster and faster record-breaking machines as World War II approached. In 1935, on a 750 cc ohv model developing 95 bhp, Henne reached 256.50 km/h (159.1 mph), but that was about as far as the 750 could be taken. The British were still in the record-breaking duel, and, to stay ahead, BMW in 1936 brought out its secret weapon – an ohc supercharged nitro-burning 750 with streamlining, developing 108 bhp. With it, Henne managed a staggering 279.50 km/h (173.675 mph).

Possibly this record of success convinced BMW that the time was ripe to try to reach new markets, for in 1935 the first BMW was imported into England. It was a 750 cc sv in a pressed-steel frame, with telescopic forks, which was a very advanced feature in England in the mid '30s. A more standard tubular frame was introduced for 1936, and the 750 remained virtually unaltered until production switched to military vehicles with the outbreak of war.

BMW's wartime efforts are worthy of comment for, while a variety

of English manufacturers produced motorcycles designed primarily for dispatch riding, the German company developed an effective fighting machine. As well as solos, a sidecar outfit appeared, powered by the 750 cc engine. This was capable of carrying three people plus equipment at around 95 km/h (60 mph). The design load was about three-quarters of a tonne, but the outfit often carried over a tonne. Again, unlike Allied equivalents, the sidecar could carry a machine-gun which helped to make this a devastating mobile weapon. So successful was it that, as early as 1942, BMW employed more than 77,000 workers.

The standard models were joined after the war by the 28 bhp R67 ohv 600 cc model in 1951, the same year that Germany was re-admitted to the *FIM*. Any hopes of easy sporting victory were dashed, however, with the ban on nitro fuels and supercharging. BMW's pre-war racers had relied on speed rather than handling. With the new regulations the ohc 500 was by no means the fastest racer around. It developed only 50 bhp, compared with 70 bhp from the pre-war models, and although roadster sales continued to flourish – the 100,000th model was sold in 1953 – racing activities were limited.

In 1954 BMWs suddenly became popular with sidecar racers. Superseding Norton, whose bikes had successfully pulled chairs to many world-class victories since the late '40s, BMW outfits were now supreme. For the next 20 years, apart from Florian Camathias on the Gilera-four in 1964, and Helmut Fath on his in-line four URS in 1968, virtually every major international sidecar road race was won by a BMW. Only by the early '70s had their dominance been weakened by newcomers such as the Konig, but they remained a force to be reckoned with.

In 1974 BMW celebrated half a century of motorcycle manufacture by winning the Maudes Trophy. Two 750s were ridden around the TT course for seven days non-stop. There were a couple of crashes, but few mechanical problems. This triumph was especially fitting, for it was here that Georg Meier became the first foreigner to win a Senior TT in 1939 – on a BMW. BMW is still developing new variations on the famous flat twin, among them the incredible 1,000 cc R100/RS introduced in 1976.

Far left: One of the most prodigious record-breakers ever, German Ernst Henne with the streamlined BMW twin. On this machine, he became the fastest man on two wheels back in 1929. At the time, the battle for record honours was waged between British vee-twins and BMW.

Below: Two top-quality machines together – the 900 cc BMW from Germany and Italy's 850 cc Moto Guzzi. The Moto Guzzi, like the BMW, features an electric starter, but its engine was originally designed for a small car and later developed for motorcycle use.

Left: Perhaps the most complex racing engine ever built, the Moto Guzzi Vee 8 of the 1950s is still remembered by many enthusiasts as much for its fantastic exhaust scream as for its performance. The motorcycle shown competed in the 1957 Isle of Man TT.

MOTO GUZZI

Although arriving relatively late on the motorcycle scene, the Italian Moto Guzzi company, founded in 1921, soon brought their machines to the attention of the public by a fantastic series of racing successes on tracks all over Europe. Brains behind the company, the brilliant designer Carlo Guzzi was a great man for experimentation. Although he was clearly a devotee of the flat, single-cylinder design, he tried many forms of valve lay-out in the early years, producing 250 cc and 500 cc machines with inlet-over-exhaust, overhead-valve and overhead-camshaft systems.

The flat, single-cylinder design survived until after World War II, when an entirely new range of machine was laid down. This included no fewer than 10 models, of two- and four-stroke type and all under 250 cc.

Guzzi's big-bike comeback of the 1960s featured a vee-twin car engine set across the frame. This machine soon made itself a name as an effortless high-speed tourer. The potential of the model influenced racers and tuners throughout Europe, and soon many special models were to be seen in production and long-distance races. The development was picked up by the factory, which soon came out with its own production racing models, raising the capacity from its original 750 cc to over 800 cc. One such model was named Le Mans, after the company's success in the famous French endurance race.

But, despite a series of successful roadster machines, it is for its racing models that the company is best known. Through the years these included supercharged 250 cc singles and a series of unblown models in the 250 cc, 350 cc and 500 cc classes. Less orthodox models included a wide-angle vee twin and even a four-cylinder special raced in the early 1950s.

But the engineering and designing skill of Carlo Guzzi was perhaps best shown in the monster he built in 1956. This was a 500 cc racer with eight cylinders. Those who saw the model race still speak in awe of its complexity and the fearful sound it made. The story has it that when the machine made a pit stop at the TT races, the only way the mechanics could discover which sparking plug was misfiring was to place one finger in turn on each exhaust pipe – the finger that was not blistered indicated the faulty plug.

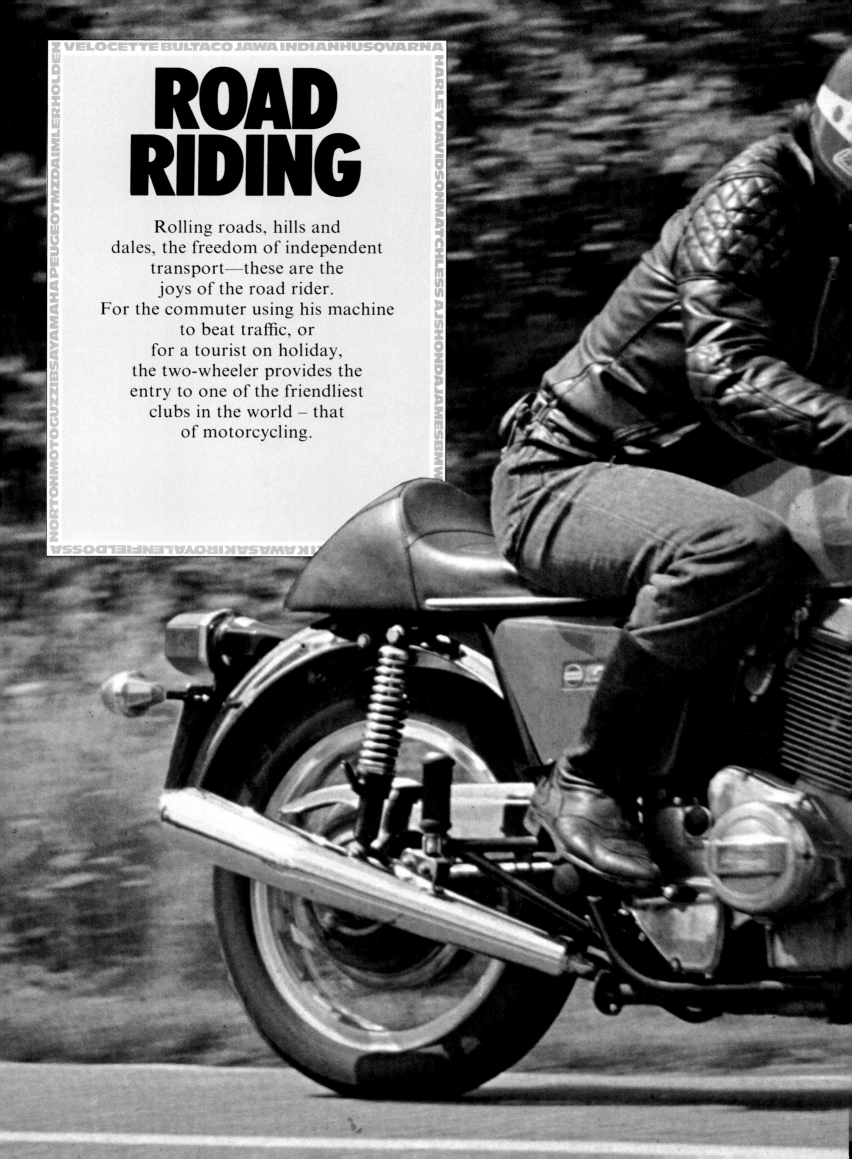

ROAD RIDING

Rolling roads, hills and
dales, the freedom of independent
transport—these are the
joys of the road rider.
For the commuter using his machine
to beat traffic, or
for a tourist on holiday,
the two-wheeler provides the
entry to one of the friendliest
clubs in the world – that
of motorcycling.

The road-riding motorcyclist can easily be slotted into one of three categories – the economy-minded commuter, the touring enthusiast and the man who sees his machine as a status symbol. Since the mid 1960s there has been an unprecedented rise in the demand for machines to fit all three categories – a demand not even equalled by the immediate post-war boom in cheap transport.

Without a doubt the phenomenal rise in world-wide registrations for small-capacity machines has followed the startling rise in fuel costs in almost every country. These costs, mirrored in public transport fares, have led to tens of thousands of commuters taking low-powered bikes as a means of getting from home to work and back. And, as governments hit by recession cut down on road-development programmes, the small motorcycle has become the only practical way of commuting on overcrowded thoroughfares.

Meanwhile, in the mid 1960s, the new range of vehicles initiated in Japan made long-distance work more feasible. Gone was the stigma of the noisy, oil-covered, temperamental machine, for you could now buy a quiet, refined, clean, gaily-coloured motorcycle that looked at home in the parking lot of any high-class hotel.

Throughout the world, manufacturers clamoured to jump on the bandwagon. All found it impossible to specialize in one type of model and most followed Honda's lead in Japan by providing the potential customer with a choice ranging from a utility moped capable of returning 70 km/l (200 mpg), through speedy yet economical tourers, to full-blooded, super-complex, multi-cylinder machines which, if not economical, certainly provided the ego trip and performances previously only associated with the most exotic sports cars.

In choosing a road machine a rider is thus faced with a bewildering selection of makes, models and varieties. The only way in which he can decide is to take a cold, hard look at the job that his machine will have to do. A rider who simply needs a motorcycle to take him a few kilometres and back each day has no need for a fierce, difficult-in-traffic, high-speed sportster. He will probably be quite happy with a 50 cc moped or even a 100 cc lightweight motorcycle. If our commuter wants to make the odd weekend trip as well, he can choose between many models of up to 250 cc. For longish trips, especially with a pillion passenger, a 350 to 500 cc machine might be more suitable. When you enter the realm of the over-500 cc machine you are considering the needs of the sportsman, or long-distance, high-speed tourist. This type of rider realizes he may seldom get the chance to achieve his mount's potential top speed of, perhaps, around 210 km/h (130 mph). But he knows his vehicle will carry him vast distances at about 110 km/h (70 mph) with the engine hardly working at all.

The most basic decision facing the prospective purchaser of a modern machine is whether to opt for a two-stroke or four-stroke design. While most manufacturers have opted for two-stroke engines for their small-capacity machines, Honda has gone along the four-stroke route, citing fuel economy as one justification for using the more complex of the two designs. The old two-stroke's bugbear was that fuel had to be mixed with oil at the service station. This problem has been banished, for most two-stroke designs now feature a separate oil tank and mixing occurs automatically within the carburettor. But the very fact that oil is burnt with the petrol may now be heralding the two-stroke's downfall. Without doubt the two-stroke engine produces more noxious exhaust emissions than its four-stroke counterpart, and the resulting air pollution is provoking protests from the world's ecological pressure groups. One day, then, the two-stroke may be all but outlawed from many Western countries. True, technologists can fit emission-control equipment to cars, but the sheer size of the components needed and the power loss they produce make such devices useless for motorcycles – at least those of present-day designs.

Yet another obvious decision that a prospective purchaser must make is whether to opt for a super-sophisticated but relatively expensive design or to go for the cheaper, more traditional machine still being marketed by Iron-Curtain countries such as Czechoslovakia, East Germany and Russia. The Eastern bloc models certainly represent good value for money, but they lag behind Western motor-

Previous pages: Part of a professional road tester's lot is to sample such machines as this exotic 1,000 cc three-cylinder Laverda Jota – a road version of a bike built for competition in the ever-growing number of long-distance endurance races on the Continent.

Above: Highlight of the touring year for many hardened enthusiasts is the annual get-together in West Germany for the Elephant Rally. Snow storms, icy roads and freezing conditions make no difference to the rallyists, who camp out for two nights just to meet other bike fans and talk about their hobby.

cycle technology and lack the charisma of Japan's mechanical marvels. But for the motorcyclist seeking cheap, reliable transport rather than high performance, these bikes represent a very real saving in initial outlay.

Vastly increased leisure time, the international fuel situation and a desire for person freedom of transport have all had a lot to do with the surging rise in motorcycle sales. Yet probably nothing has done more to make the motorcycle socially acceptable than the fact that manufacturers of riding apparel have at last caught up with fashion. Until relatively few years ago the choice of riding wear was limited and unbecoming. There was an ankle-length coat that had to be buckled around the knees and did little to protect the lower part of the body. Or you could have had a heavyweight, plastic, two-piece riding suit that soon wear-hardened and cracked. The ultimate was a waxed linen suit. But this only temporarily repelled the elements. Moreover it left traces of its black wax covering on any pale object that the wearer touched. (Like Mr Ford's famous Model T, the choice of colours was usually limited to black.) Now, an increased use of man-made fibres and pliable plastic-based materials has seen the birth of a new generation of riding suits. Riders today have a choice of gaily coloured gear that is not only clean but provides better weather protection than its predecessors did. It also renders the wearer less

liable to accidents, for the brightly coloured suits are much more easily seen, especially at night, than the drab wear of years gone by.

Nowadays the ankle-length coats have all but disappeared. They are almost museum pieces, receiving an airing only when members of vintage and veteran collectors' clubs take part in rallies on their elderly machines.

The waxed linen suit still has its devotees, but to be kept in top fettle it needs periodic re-waxing – a messy job not to be attempted on the living-room carpet. Trials riders are the suit's chief advocates: they value the protection it affords to motorcyclists as they crash through brambles in a forest.

The present-day motorcyclist has a wide choice of wearing apparel, and many people opt for at least two suits to match different weather conditions. In the dry, a lightweight nylon oversuit is sufficient protection, and it has the advantage of being easily packed and stored in the pannier box of the touring machine when not in use. For wet and cold conditions, the modern-day plastic-based suit has the advantage of being 100 per cent waterproof and of providing a good thermal barrier between the rider and the elements. Although it is common in hot climates to see motorcyclists riding in shirt-sleeves or even bare-chested, the practice has little to commend it. Even the most trivial spill can turn nasty if there is no protection between the rider and the road surface.

For the same reason the use of a crash helmet is becoming universally accepted. Throughout Britain, many countries in Europe and most states in America, wearing a crash helmet is obligatory. Again, technology has advanced the design of helmets since the early 1960s. Motorcycle manufacturers have come into line by providing pro-helmet publicity and many add a helmet lock to the basic design of a machine so that the headwear can be firmly secured to the machine when left by the rider. Also with safety in mind, there is little argument against wearing goggles or a visor to protect the eyes. The

current vogue for space-type, fully-enveloping helmets with an integral chin bar favours the use of a wrap-around visor screen, although some such visors are made from materials that can easily scratch and need regular replacement. Misting is the main snag with a visor or goggles, but there are several proprietory preparations for treating the glass or perspex to avoid this problem.

Other commonsense aids to safety are strong boots that support the ankles, and gloves that help prevent abrasion damage in the event of a spill. With gloves there is a choice between the conventional item and the gauntlet. Many long-distance riders prefer the gauntlet, which has fewer seams, a fact that helps to make it particularly warm and waterproof. But others maintain that hands encased in gauntlets have less feel for the controls than hands enclosed in ordinary gloves. Perhaps the best compromise is a pair of good leather gloves with gauntlet overmitts for really nasty weather.

Adequate dress, however, is not itself a passport to the open road. There are legal obligations to be met. These vary from country to country. In some parts of Europe a 15 year old may ride a low-powered moped without buying a licence or taking a test. In Britain, though, there is a graduated scheme whereby 16 year olds may ride mopeds, and 17 year olds may ride full motorcycles, but of no more than 250 cc until the riders have passed a proficiency test.

There are various ways of learning to ride. For instance, driving schools cater for would-be motorcyclists on a commercial basis and, in Britain, local councils help support training schemes aimed at giving young motorcyclists a grounding in road safety and maintenance before they take their government-supervised driving test. Then, too, many motorcycle clubs run training schemes.

A beginner can even teach himself to ride, perhaps with the aid of an experienced friend. But obviously this is best done in the confines of a secluded car park where the inevitable training mistakes can take place without danger to the rider or other road users.

The greatest asset to any rider is confidence in himself and in his machine. Any experienced racers man taking over a new model assures himself that he is fully comfortable before he sets off. First, he simply sits on the machine, judging the positions of controls. Then he has these altered slightly to meet his own requirements. An experienced man also takes it easy when riding a strange model. He tests the potential of its brakes long before evaluating speed and acceleration. He knows it is the front brake, universally operated by the right-hand handle-bar lever, that provides most of his retardation. He knows, too, that braking throws much of the weight of the bike and rider to the front of the machine. The current vogue is to fit disc front brakes to powerful machines, as discs have great stopping power and water tends to leave them unaffected. But, in the wet, the seasoned rider treats the front brake with special caution. This is because he remembers that the coefficient of friction between tyre and road reduces dramatically in rain – especially during a shower after a prolonged dry spell when the combination of water and traffic film provides an extremely slippery surface. In the wet, then, he relies slightly more on the back brake, for a rear-wheel skid is far easier to control than locking of the front wheel. In the wet, in fact, everything will be done in a more calculatedly gentle and progressive manner than in dry weather. Corners, for example, must be taken slowly enough to prevent the bike canting over as far as it will safely tilt in dry conditions.

So far we have considered the road rider and his basic machine. But many riders add additional equipment to their bikes. Among such 'extras' by far the largest item is a sidecar. Once the favourite means of family transport for the working man, the sidecar outfit all but vanished in the 1960s, but it has made a come-back with the sporting set. Now that large-capacity machines approach small cars in cost the sidecar outfit is no longer a cheap way of transporting the family, but because of its design it presents a series of unique riding challenges to its owner. For, although a solo will quite happily follow a given line when banked for a corner, a sidecar has to be *driven* around bends, much more so than a car. In most cars the rear wheels drive and the front wheels steer, but on a sidecar outfit things are more complicated. One wheel at the front, off-set from the centre-line of the machine does the steering; another, similarly placed at the rear, provides the drive; but the third wheel, serving merely as a prop, is a passenger about a metre (three feet) to one side of the bike.

The main problem is that the drive of the rear wheel is always trying to send the machine around the sidecar wheel while this produces drag to one side. To counteract this, the rider leans the motorcycle away from the sidecar, giving the sidecar wheel a degree of 'toe in', so that it points slightly toward the front wheel of the machine. Theoretically, on a flat, straight road, a perfectly set-up outfit would proceed in a straight line without handle-bar effort. But few straight roads are flat. Most have cambers, and even a slight slope requires continual steering correction.

Turning also calls for special care. Take, as an example, turning an outfit where the sidecar is positioned to the right of the machine – the usual set-up in countries where traffic keeps to the right of a road. In this case a left-hand turn would involve the use of braking power, either from the machine's brakes or from retardation provided by closing the throttle. This, in effect, slows the rear wheel of the machine and allows the free-running sidecar wheel to run around it. On a right-hand turn, the motorcycle has to travel in a greater arc than the sidecar wheel and you have to accelerate to complete the manoeuvre with a minimum of steering effort.

It has been said, with some degree of truth, that no one who rides a sidecar has not had some form of crash. And that prang has usually taken place within the first few kilometres. This is not surprising. The relative weight of the motorcycle and lightness of the sidecar make a rider used to solo travel feel that the sidecar wheel is trying to lift up off the road. To counter this he almost automatically turns the bike's front wheel away from the sidecar, and bang! The outfit overturns. Anticipating this problem an experienced sidecar rider teaching a

Left: It's not only the racers that are attracted to the Isle of Man TT. Ordinary road-riding bike lovers disembark from the ferry to take part in a motorcycle fest.

Above right: Motorcycles provide sturdy service to police forces around the world. Perhaps most famous of all is the American motorcycle policeman on his Harley-Davidson.

novice will load the sidecar with boxes of tools, bricks or even a blacksmith's anvil. As the novice gains experience, the weights can be slowly reduced until all are gone and the rider can sample the unique thrills that come from skilled handling of one of the most difficult machines to ride.

The sidecar is just one of many possible extras. Thanks to Japanese influence, some are now automatically included on sophisticated models. Electric starters, mirrors and winking indicators – now considered standard equipment – were virtually unheard of in the early 1960s.

Even today, though, few motorcycles come equipped to carry luggage. But accessory firms have noted this omission and produced a considerable range of pannier and top-box equipment. Theoretically, the best position to carry camping gear or any other luggage on a motorcycle is as low and as near the centre-line of the machine as possible. But this is where the engine goes. A compromise is therefore reached. There are, in effect, three positions where you can put your luggage: above the fuel tank, on a platform behind the dual seat, and in pannier boxes straddling the rear wheel. The rear-mounted carrier behind the rider, for long the favourite position for a grid-mounted top box, can often hamper mounting and dismounting. Moreover, much weight carried there tends to make the motorcycle unwieldy on corners, and is especially risky in wet weather as it reduces the weight percentage on the all-important front wheel. Pannier bags astride the rear wheel certainly get the weight lower down, but a prospective purchaser of such equipment should check that the mounting brackets are sturdy and that such components need not be fitted in a way that hinders maintenance, for instance removal of the rear wheel following a puncture. Large-capacity tank-top bags are a fairly recent innovation but already much in favour in many countries. Riders find that, properly loaded, such a bag helps support

the rider's chest, thus relieving pressure on his arms over long-distance rides.

Few machines are designed with weather-protecting fairings, but you can buy these extras in many styles and colours; there is something here for virtually every machine on the market. Their main advantages are twofold: they give a considerable degree of weather protection, especially at speed, and their streamlined profiles add marginally to the performance and fuel economy of the machines. But they have the twin disadvantages of reducing accessibility and increasing engine noise heard by the rider, the fairings acting as a sound box and throwing back noise.

Even the best-made and best-equipped machines need maintenance. Before the mid 1960s the owner of a motorcycle was usually something of a mechanic, but the new breed of enthusiast is happier to leave routine servicing to a specialist. The real reason for this is increased complexity of design. With the simple single- and even twin-cylinder designs of the early '60s it was fairly easy to do most jobs – even most major work – in a home garage. But specialist tools and skills are needed for a large number of the tasks carried out on a modern type of bike. For example, it took the average owner little more than 10 minutes to tune the carburettor on his single-cylinder machine, but a skilled mechanic, using complex vacuum instruments, needs considerably longer to set the carburettors on something as involved as a four-cylinder Honda or Kawasaki. Also, because of the intricate engineering involved, the current generation of highly stressed, high-revving, multi-cylinder engines needs considerably more servicing than its 'go on forever' predecessors.

The modern motorcycle provides efficient and trouble-free use, but only if servicing is religiously adhered to. And while it is still possible for the home mechanic to perform certain tasks on his modern machine, many jobs are best left to the expert.

TRIALS

The slowest, but perhaps
the most mentally demanding of
all motorcycle sports,
trials riding, at club or
international level, goes back
to the very basics of
competition. Men and machines
pit themselves against
mud, roots, rocks, climbs,
sand and water – every hazard
that nature can conjure up.

Given time, professionalism will enter any branch of any sport. But the last aspect of the great two-wheel game to attract big money was the old English competition, trials. Basically, trials involve a rider surmounting a series of obstacles, and a scoring system for assessing his performance. If the competitor succeeds in crossing, say a rocky stream bed, without stopping and without putting his feet to the ground, he is said to have cleaned the section and no penalty marks are debited against his name. Should he require a steady prod with one foot he incurs a single mark. Another dab to the ground will add another point, and a need for a further piece of footwork brings his adverse score to three. Should the worse happen and the rider stop, fall, or stray outside the boundaries of the hazard he gets the maximum of five marks. At the end of the day's run each contestant has his total score assessed and the man with the fewest marks comes out the winner.

In the early days of trials – and it's a sport that dates back to the start of motorcycling – the machines were basically lightened roadsters with sports tyres for added grip. And it was here that big, British, single-cylinder machines held a virtual monopoly, their good torque and low-down pulling power making up for any weight disadvantage. Things really began to change in the 1950s at the hands of two small British companies. Dot (which could trace its ancestry back to the early days of the industry) and Greeves (an offshoot of an invalid-carriage company) started to market highly developed 200 and 250 cc two-strokes based on the proprietary Villiers engine. Greeves went further than Dot, adding its own engine parts, until virtually the entire power plant was the product of this small company. And the small British two-strokes may well have dominated trials events (then still not booming outside Britain) had it not been for one man's virtual monopoly of the awards list. He was Irishman Sammy Miller who worked for the BSA company. Miller had developed a 500 cc Ariel – originally produced by the BSA offshoot – into a highly competitive machine, and on this he kept the two-strokes at bay, and undoubtedly helped prolong the life of the large-capacity four-stroke trials machine.

But in the early 1960s even Sammy Miller could read the writing on the wall, and after some super-secret negotiations with the small Spanish Bultaco factory, announced to a stunned motorcycle world that he was pensioning off the old Ariel and in future would campaign on a 250 cc two-stroke. The Bultaco's initial outing was a disaster. Cynics nodded their heads wisely and announced that Sammy had made the biggest blunder of his career. But not so. A week later he was back, with the bugs ironed out of the Bultaco, to begin a new success story just as distinguished as that which he had written with his Ariel. Miller's Bultaco changed the face of trials overnight. Orders flooded in for replicas and Bultaco was soon flat out attempting to keep up. It was, therefore, no surprise when Bultaco's chief Spanish rival, Montesa, produced a similar machine – this time with the aid of ex-Greeves rider Don Smith. A third Barcelona factory came close behind, well publicized by Mick Andrews who forsook his big-capacity AJS to develop a 250 cc Ossa.

The trials market soon grew out of all expectation. Heralded by demonstration tours throughout America, Miller, Andrews and Smith brought trials riding to the States and soon a new and vast demand for trials machines was blossoming. Now the Japanese moved in, and did so in the biggest possible way. Yamaha spearheaded the attack, tempting Andrews away from Ossa to produce a machine that must hold the record for the most expensive trials bike development. Andrews commuted between Britain and Japan, finalizing the model, and when it at last burst on the European scene it arrived with a bevy of Japanese technicians assessing its performance at every turn.

After a row with Montesa, Smith left and was a natural choice for Kawasaki, the next Japanese production team into the market. However, Kawasaki's development programme seemed half-hearted, and by the mid 1970s the machine had yet to click with the world's top riders. Next to see the potential of the trials market was Suzuki, who obtained the services of ex-Triumph and Greeves man Gordon Farley to produce a machine. The initial model was a total failure, but, after Farley left, a new model surprisingly appeared for the 1975 season. In the hands of Nigel Birkett and John Metcalfe it chalked up

Previous page: Sometime road racer, Nick Jefferies was one of the first men to really get to grips with the Honda trials machine.

Above: Trials riding, once the poor relation of motorcycle sport on the Continent, is now taking off in a big way. This Bultaco rider is taking part in the Clamart event, one of the classic French trials.

Right: Most popular trials machine for many years, the Spanish Bultaco is produced in 125 cc, 250 cc and 325 cc sizes. Here Briton Chris Milner puts one foot to the ground for a steadying prod as he crosses a stream bed.

a fantastic series of successes. Surprisingly, that most adventurous and largest of the Japanese companies, Honda, entered the trials field last. Honda was clearly worried about the potential of the market, for to make a new model economic, the firm believed it must produce more units of that type than any other manufacturer. Honda eventually secured the services of the maestro Miller, tempting him from Bultaco. But, reminiscent of the Smith/Kawasaki deal a strange lack of determination on the manufacturer's behalf clouded the outcome and – at first at any rate – no world-class-calibre machines appeared.

Despite the formidable Japanese invasion of their stamping ground the Spanish did not despair, but hit back in two major ways. First, they embarked upon a tremendous development programme that boosted engine size on virtually all of their trials machines. Secondly, they paid out hitherto unheard-of sums to secure the world's best riders. Bultaco signed Malcolm Rathmell and Martin Lampkin, two Yorkshiremen who, between them, dominated the European scene. And when Rathmell was lured away to Montesa, the inter-factory rivalry was kept alive.

In 1976 the feet-up sport produced its biggest upset when taciturn Finn Yrjo Vesterinen beat Britain as its own game to wrench the world championship from his Bultaco team mate, Martin Lampkin. The trials world championship was then just one year old. It had been a long time in the making, for the governing body of world

motorcycle sport, the *Fédération Internationale Motocycliste,* had proved slow to grasp the popularity of trials. Indeed, only in 1966 had the federation agreed to give a series of international competitions the title of European Championship.

First to take the European title was one of the most seasoned British riders, Londoner Don Smith. Smith notched up his victory in 1967 on a Greeves. A year later, and it was Sammy Miller's turn to bring the title to Spain for Bultaco. In 1969 the trophy stayed with a Spanish manufacturer (Montesa) but this time Smith was once again the victor. The 1970s started with Miller at the top, but then Mick Andrews came in on his Ossa for two wins in '71 and '72. Bultaco snatched the title back 12 months later with the riding skill of Martin Lampkin and clung on in 1974 with Malcolm Rathmell at the helm.

When the *FIM* relented and agreed to give the event world status for the 1975/76 series, they could not have foreseen what a needle-match would result. At the final round there could have been three winners – Rathmell, Lampkin or Vesterinen. Lampkin made it, but Vesterinen was second and many said that the days of British trials dominance were well and truly numbered. They were proved right just 12 months later when Vesterinen (who lives in Belgium to be near the centre of trials activity) took the title.

The majority of trials, including those counting for the world championship, are simply one-day affairs over a course of around 50 kilometres (30 miles) and with anything up to 40 sections. But for the true hard-riding enthusiast there is no event to equal the importance or excitement of the long-distance events. Premier of these is the Scottish Six Days' Trial, running through the Western Highlands of Scotland, and now the multi-day event is catching on, with regular long-distance trials in Europe and America.

The same battle for status that was fought by the solo riders in their bid for world-championship recognition is now waged by the sidecar trials fraternity. By the mid 1970s they had an unofficial European series, but there was talk within the *FIM* of soon giving this full European status and eventually world-class recognition.

Sidecar trials, in which the passenger is as an important part of the team as the rider, saw the same evolution of machinery as the solo sport. However, with the three-wheeler outfit, the big single-cylinder four-stroke held on to supremacy for much longer, and it was not until the advent of the larger, 350 cc capacity two-strokes from Spain and Japan that the sidecars followed the solo two-stroke route.

Now trials means big business in many countries, but the loss of rough-ground venues brought about by building programmes and conservationist activity may help to change the sport dramatically within the next few years. Hitherto trials has been primarily a participator sport with little spectator attraction, only the most determined enthusiasts following the riders from section to section, often across difficult ground, to watch them perform.

It was in Sweden that people first tried out the idea of bringing trials to the spectators. A Swedish club hired an indoor arena normally used for show jumping and built a series of man-made obstacles within the ring. This first event owed more to gimmickry than anything. Riders were expected to run their machines along planks and step-ladders and over cars. It may have been good fun for the spectators but few riders showed enthusiasm. Next to try the idea was a Dutch club that went about it much more professionally. Tonnes of earth and boulders and logs were moved into a show-ring to form sections. The technique caught on, and even water splashes are now part of such indoor events.

The indoor trials has its critics who say that the events are little more than circus turns. But the crowds seem to enjoy them, and in the comfort of a warm arena can watch each rider's individual performance over every section and see his score on a master board visible to all, and such events are taking off, internationally.

Top left: Known as Charlie Custard to his friends, French Champion Charles Cootard fights to stay upright in a rocky stream bed in the Scottish Six Days Trial.

Left: Top rider and chief development man for Yamaha, Mick Andrews has European championship titles to his credit. But he performs best in long-distance events like the annual Scottish Six Days Trial held in the Western Highlands.

Right: On rocks, a bike can sometimes have a mind of its own, even when the machine is the latest of a line of works models Montesas and the rider is as experienced as Rob Edwards.

SPEEDWAY

The tracks are short,
the races often over in less
than a minute, but the action
at a speedway meeting
is on the top line.
Four determined riders on
the dope-burning, brakeless
machines fight it out
on a shale oval to the roar
of the crowds – that's what
speedway is all about.

Engines racing, exhausts roaring, chains whirring and thrashing – four, helmeted, leather-clad riders tweak the throttles of their machines behind three flimsy strips of elastic that form the tapes.

About to live with the riders every second of the race to come, the enthusiastic crowd grows restive. Murmured support switches to shouts of encouragement, stopping abruptly as the tapes fly skywards. Riders' backs straighten as clutches are dropped, and four sprays of shale are spat out by spinning wheels as the contestants make their race for the first bend.

Spectator cheering rises to a crescendo as the riders, sometimes brushing against one another, jostle for the best line, each urging his bike farther forward until the slower starters are forced to break off the engagement. Four high-speed, broadsiding, shale-showering laps follow as the slower starters endeavour to make up lost ground and overtake, on the inside or the outside, to come from the back.

That's speedway: most professional of the motorcycle sports, where the winner takes everything – prize money, honour, adulation, applause and prestige – the losers, nothing – only the knowledge that they tried their darnedest and there's always tomorrow.

Speedway has thrived, survived rough periods and thrived again over more than half a century. During that time dirt racing, as the sport was first known, has radically changed, though it has always kept a following of enthusiastic and appreciative fans.

The honour of originating speedway goes to the Americans, who raced around oval, horse-trotting tracks, all over the States. They also competed on board tracks, but it was the sight of early aces such as Shrimp Burns pushing 1,000 cc machines flat-out over rough dirt tracks, that captured the public's thrill-seeking attention. Such was the power and weight of the bikes (Harley-Davidson and Indian were two prominent manufacturers) that corners were negotiated bolt upright. But following many accidents, several of them fatal, engines had been limited to 500 cc by the early 1920s. These smaller, lighter machines induced riders to broadside so as to maintain speed through the corners.

The Americans taught the Australians the style on a visit Down Under in the mid 1920s. Aussies had previously raced on concrete or grass tracks. Then Johnnie Hoskins – later to become the most famous speedway promoter of all time – had cinders laid on the Maitland track to give a loose surface and encourage the new style. The sport blossomed, expanded and flourished. At the first 0.4 km (quarter-mile) track at Brisbane, in 1926, Cecil Brown instigated a further development – the leg-trailing style.

Word of the exciting new craze reached Britain and there the call went up for similar events. The Camberley Club became first to organize a dirt track meeting, on 7th May, 1927. But the track consisted of deep sand and, of all things, riders circulated clockwise . . . the wrong way. A proper dirt track event was staged the following month in Manchester, at Droylesden.

However, the occasion now celebrated as the true birth of British speedway took place near London in February, 1928. Australians were key figures, among them Johnny Hoskins and A. J. Hunting, founder of the Brisbane quarter-miler.

By 1976 Britain had the strongest and best-run speedway league in the world, but the sport of speedway was also strong in Sweden, Poland, Russia, Australia and New Zealand, with Denmark, West Germany and America taking an ever increasing interest.

America, the originator of the game, has until recently preferred to look inward, running meetings under the jurisdiction of its own Amateur Motorcycle Association. Its last, and only, world champion was Jack Milne in 1937. But since America's recent shift in outlook and affiliation to the *Fédération Internationale Motocycliste*, the world governing body, things have changed. Moreover Scott Autrey, an England-based Californian, who rides for Exeter, in 1976 became the first American to qualify for a world final for many years. Nucleus of the European-style speedway revival west of the Atlantic is the Pacific Coast state of California.

Since World War II, world championships have been dominated by two nations – New Zealand and Sweden. Head and shoulders above

their rivals stand Sweden's Ove Fundin, winner of a record five championships, closely followed by Kiwis' Ivan Mauger (only man to have clinched three successive victories: 1968-70) and Barry Briggs, each with four titles. With two wins apiece are New Zealander Ronnie Moore, Denmark's Ole Olsen and the late Peter Craven of England. Highlighting England's return to individual big-time speedway, 22-year-old Belle Vue star Peter Collins won his first world championship in 1976, 14 years since Craven's had brought England's last success.

In the early days a whole host of machines was tried on the dirt tracks – very much roadsters stripped of lights and accessories, with handlebars turned down. AJS, BSA, Harley-Davidson, Scott, Douglas, Indian, Rudge . . . think of a machine and somebody, somewhere raced it on dirt. Harley-Davidson's 350 cc single-cylinder Peashooter, the 500 cc Rudge, and Douglas in-line, horizontally opposed twin were to become famous on the dirt, the latter particularly spectacular and suitable for the leg-trailing school. However, it was the power characteristics of the 500 cc JAP single-engine, raced foot-forward in a short-wheelbase frame, that proved to be superior, so much so that it was the world's number-one machine for close to 40 years, only giving way to the shorter stroke, Czech-made Eso (later renamed Jawa) in the mid 1960s.

The Jawa's reign, with a two-valve engine, was far shorter. This was largely because the British company of Weslake, at Rye in Sussex, introduced a four-valve engine to speedway in March, 1975, after a successful grass-track debut at Lydden, Kent, in October 1974. The Weslake rocketed to the forefront overnight. Ridden by John Louis, the engine won the British Championship at Coventry and later the same season came third in the world final, behind Ole Olsen and Swede Anders Michanek.

The four-valver revolutionized modern speedway with its revitalized machinery. Notable four-valve competition now came from Neil Street and his four-valve, the Swedish ERM, and Jawa, which also made an end-of-1976-season comeback with its own four-valve. Works rider Ivan Mauger won the world 1,000 metre (3,280 feet) sand-track final on it in its racing debut, and Ole Olsen, the British

Previous pages: All the action of the speedway scene as Englishman John Louis broadsides his 500 cc Jawa to keep ahead of Swedish ace Bernt Persson. Riders from New Zealand, Australia, England and Sweden provide most of the world's top men.

Above: An offshoot of speedway, sand racing can provide even more spectacle. Look closely at the picture, for this is a sidecar with the driver throwing the banked outfit hard into a left-hand bend during a West German meeting.

Top right: Jerzy Rembas of Poland tries too hard at the start as the tapes go up and will have to throttle back or chance his 500 cc Eso rearing up and throwing him onto the cinders.

Bottom right: Things can get pretty crowded during the hustle of the first corner at a speedway meeting, but no-one is going to back off on the throttle for there are valuable team points and prize money at stake.

League Divisional One Rider's Final. But most British-based riders were now racing Weslakes, and the engine's meteoric rise to success climaxed in September 1976, in Poland, where factory riders Peter Collins and 1976 British champion Malcolm Simmons finished first and second in the world final.

It's the accelerative power of the four-valvers that makes these so successful. Otherwise they resemble conventional speedway engines, running as they do on methanol not petrol, and producing 55-60 bhp. Incidentally, speedway bikes have just two controls: a clutch lever and throttle. That's right, no gearbox – a countershaft instead, and for safety reasons, no brakes!

Let's now briefly see how speedway racing actually operates. A speedway team consists of seven members. The best three are called *heat leaders*, the next two are *second strings*, and there are two *reserves*. Heat leaders and second strings have four rides each in a normal league match of 13 races or heats. Reserves rate three scheduled rides but may replace team-mates in poor form or suffering machine trouble. If a team trails by six or more points after the fourth race, its manager may substitute one of his best men – a rule devised to keep competition hot. Riders are identified by helmet covers.

From a standing start, contestants race anti-clockwise over four laps of an oval, shale-carpeted circuit of about 350 metres (about

380 yards). Beneath shale 2.5-5 centimetres (1-2 inches) deep is hardcore, and many hours are spent by groundsmen rolling, racking, smoothing and watering a track to mould it into first-class condition before a meeting.

Finishing order and times are announced after each race so that spectators can keep race programmes up to date. For many people, filling in their own programme is an important part of the proceedings. Riders gain three points for a win, two for second place, and one for third – whether a league match or individual contest is involved. They also get a cash sum for each point scored as well as travel expenses and start money. Top stars also net appearance payments.

Little sister of speedway is grass-track, a sport rapidly gaining favour in Europe. Machines are similar to those of speedway, many of them armed with Eso and JAP engines for the 500 cc class. But, whereas speedway bikes lack brakes entirely, grass-track models make some concession to the need for stopping. So similar are the two sports that many riders excel in both, for grass-track venues – although slightly bumpier than those of speedway – call for basically the same techniques. To deal with the bumps and longer circuits, grass-track machines normally have rear springing and larger capacity fuel tanks.

But it is in the offshoots of grass-track racing that novelty really comes into its own. For the 250 cc class (all speedway machines,

incidentally, are now of 500 cc capacity) – many engines have been tried with varying success. In sidecar grass-track racing, the most powerful racing machines around take part. Many grass-track sidecar outfits are powered with virtually road-racing engines, but while road racing carries capacity restrictions, sidecar racing is virtually wide open. Add to large engines rules that allow supercharging and the use of high-performance fuels, and the power produced by the top models is truly startling.

Previous pages: Is there any reason to doubt the thrills of speedway with action like this? Four riders on similar machines must rely on skill and daring to force their way through to the front. Accidents are common, but serious injury is rare indeed.

Top: The reason for the angle at which these riders have their machines is that they are taking part in yet another speedway off-shoot – ice racing – with huge spikes sticking out of their tyres.

Right: Close-up on the spikes. The mechanic is warming the engine with a blowlamp – the only way it can be made to start in sub-zero temperatures.

ROAD RACING

The biggest cash prizes in
motor-cycle sport are
reserved for the road-racers,
the men who risk their
lives at speeds others only
dream of, on circuits
all over the world.
Road racing today is big
business and the men
who race and win are the
giants of the sport.

It is only human nature that a man should want to demonstrate his prowess, be it muscular or mechanical, in competition with his fellows. Early man no doubt held spear-throwing contests. Early motorcyclists betook themselves and their machines to established cycle racing venues such as the Parc au Princes track in Paris, or Crystal Palace, Canning Town and Aston Villa in England. Such tracks were often floored with wooden boards and slightly banked at turns. The races held there were usually two-man challenge matches involving such giants of the day as Harry and Charlie Collier (sons of the founder of the Matchless company), Sam Wright and Harry Martin with their MMC-powered Excelsiors, and the Tessier brothers with their Croydon-built Bat-JAPs.

But it was on the Continent that the sport really flourished in the early 1900s. There, tracks were bigger and faster than in Britain, and the machines evolved by French and Austrian factories, in particular, packed more and more power into their spidery frames by the simple device of incorporating bigger and still bigger engines. Frankly, these machines were freaks, with tremendous wheelbases, and enormous engines poking up between the twin top tubes of the frames. One such monster was the vee-four Clement. Another, seen at the Parc au Princes track, required two men to drive it – one to steer, and the other, riding pillion, to operate the controls. Nevertheless, the building of such machinery did give the Continental factories initial impetus. They were learning all the while, and they were to learn still more from the races held over open roads in France – the Paris-Bordeaux, Paris-Madrid, Paris-Vienna, and so on.

With car racing as a precedent, the Isle of Man was chosen in 1905 as the venue for the *Coupe Internationale* British team selection tests. At first, it was suggested that for these, too, the hill climb after passing through Ramsey should be included, but there was an outcry from the motorcycle manufacturers. Machines for the *Coupe Internationale* races, they said, were belt drive and single geared, and incapable of tackling such a ferocious gradient. Instead, the tests were conducted over the long Ballamodha Straight, running south from Foxdale. But they did much for the sport, internationally. British men and machines proved completely outclassed, but claimed that Continental makers had twisted the rules to ensure their own success.

The dispute reached a climax with the 1906 *Coupe Internationale* races, held in Austria, where the host nation's team rode Puch vee-twins. Cheating was blatant, and the Internationale jury was forced to act when, on a tour of inspection during the race, it came upon a Puch works car – which, of course, had no right to be on the circuit – bowling along merrily, stuffed to the gunwales with spares, tyres, and works mechanics.

Such was the subsequent controversy that the *Coupe Internationale* series was, mercifully, ended. In any case, thought the Auto-Cycle Club (forerunner of the Auto-Cycle Union), the type of racing machine that competition of this nature was developing bore little relation to the standard production bike of the day. What was needed was some kind of event to benefit the touring bike. Good idea, agreed the Marquis de Mouzilly de St. Mars, who had been Britain's jury member at the final *Coupe Internationale* race. What is more, to get such a meeting off the ground, he would donate a handsome prize – a tourist trophy. There followed considerable argument as to what constituted a touring machine as opposed to an out-and-out racing model, but eventually the Auto-Cycle Club drew up regulations whereby the winner was to be the fastest finisher in relation to a specified fuel consumption – which, looking back, appears a curious decision.

Again at odds with present attitudes, twin-cylinder machines (and here the term embraced four-in-line engines, such as the Belgian-made FN) were held inferior to single-cylinder models. Thus the twins got a concession: they had to average a minimum of only 26 km/l (75 mpg), whereas a single had to do 32 km/l (90 mpg), or better.

But at least there was no argument concerning venue. The Isle of Man people wanted the race, and were willing to close roads as necessary. So a 26 km (16 mile) lap was selected, starting from Tynwald Hill and running by way of Ballacraine and Glen Helen to Kirkmichael, where a left turn led back by the coast road to the outskirts of Peel, and so again to St. Johns. The lap had to be covered 10 times in all, but there would be a compulsory lunch break of 10 minutes for each competitor. For the period this was quite a testing circuit, as even present-day visitors to the island will know, and it included the quite formidable climb up past Sarah's Cottage on to the undulating Cronk-y-Voddee straight. But at least the Sarah's Cottage climb had one advantage: competing bikes would be travelling at only a snail's pace, probably with the rider pedalling away like fury to help the engine, so it was no problem for a helper to run alongside his man and shout instructions into his ear.

For the record, the single-cylinder winner of that first, 1907 TT race was Charlie Collier on his JAP-engined Matchless, while the Hele-Shaw Cup, for the winner of the separate twin-cylinder entry, went to Rembrandt Fowler and his Peugeot-powered Norton vee-twin. For the record, also, all bar two Triumph machines were equipped with an auxiliary pedalling mechanism. That, reckoned the organizers, gave some riders an unfair advantage and, if the tourist machine was to get anywhere at all, it should do so on its own mechanical merits. For 1908, therefore, pedalling gear was banned. The fuel-consumption element was retained for several more years and, again on the assumption that twins were inferior, such engines were allowed to be of slightly larger capacity than the corresponding singles.

Back on the British mainland another development was taking place, and this was to have far-reaching consequences. At Weybridge, Surrey, Mr H. F. Locke-King was busily constructing a vast concrete race track, with steeply banked bends, on his own private estate. This was Brooklands, soon to become the home of the British Motor Cycle Racing Club, and of a select coterie of tuners and record-attempters. Indeed, the first race ever held at the brand-new track, in 1908, involved only two motorcycles: a Vindec ridden by Oscar Bickford, and a Triumph piloted by Gordon McMinnies. McMinnies won and, thereby, became the first-ever victor of a Brooklands race. But in truth this was a private duel, enacted a few weeks before the track's official opening.

Though the short 26 kilometre (16 mile) TT lap served its purpose for a while, in 1911 came a move to the full mountain course, more or less as it is today except that the Governor's Bridge and Glen-crutchery Road sections were not used. Instead, competitors swung right at the top of Cronk-ny-Mona rise, to travel by way of Willaston to the top of Bray Hill. With this move, race-machine development

Previous pages: Although road racing has always provided thrills, it is only in recent years that colour and spectacle have come to the sport. Multicoloured leathers, bikes and helmets add to the excitement.

Right: The fastest circuit in the world and the start of the 1976 250 cc championship race at Spa Francorchamps in Belgium. For the tens of thousands of spectators, the annual Spa meeting, usually bathed in sunshine, is the high point of their racing year.

Below: The flag is down and riders bump start their machines for a world 250 cc championship round in Finland in 1976. Only in production races do riders use kick or electric starters.

went into top gear – and literally so, because the formidable climb out of Ramsey hastened the coming of the countershaft gearbox, with consequent benefit to roadster machines, too.

A Junior TT race was added to the programme, with the object of encouraging development of the smaller type of machine. But there was also an expression of reactionary thought, in that two-strokes – which fired twice as often as corresponding four-strokes and, therefore, ought to have been more powerful – had to contend with an arbitrary 'equalizing factor' of 1.32 to 1. Under this formula, a 450 cc Scott became, in theory at least, 594 cc.

After peace arrived in 1918, road racing moved into a new phase. There were dozens of new manufacturers eager to have a go, and JAP and Blackburn were ready to supply them with reasonably competitive engines. For 1920, the Isle of Man TT course took on its final 60.75 km (37.75 mile) form. And, if Brooklands didn't exactly attract thousands of spectators (the slogan was 'The right crowd and no crowding', and race meetings were conveniently held on Wednesday afternoons), the track at least encouraged the new breed of racing rider who had in many cases earned his motorcycling spurs as a dispatch rider on the Western Front. But Brooklands had one great problem. It was built in the wrong place, and the organizers suffered continual complaints from the householders surrounding the track. In an effort to appease the residents, racing was restricted to eight hours a day, and motorcycles had to be fitted with the huge, flat, lozenge-shaped silencer and fishtail known generally as the 'Brooklands Can'. As might be expected, replicas of the Brooklands Can were soon available from trendier motorcycle shops up and down the country, and the pseudo-sporty boys rushed to buy.

Brooklands became the haunt of would-be record-breakers, for there was no other suitable track in Britain. But the eight-hour restriction had the ludicrous result that attempts on the 24-hour record had to be carried out in spasms, the bike meanwhile being

Previous pages: For the ultimate in cornering, a rider will climb all over his machine in an effort to keep it as upright as possible. Acrobat here is multi-world champion Giacomo Agostini on a Yamaha.

Top left: Devotee of the 50 cc machine, Britain's Barry Smith at Imola, Italy on a mini Derbi.

Above: At well over 160 kilometres per hour (100 mph), you have to trust the man just in front. And that is just what Chas Mortimer is doing as he chases after Tom Heron during a 500 cc battle in Sweden.

Top right: Road racing is now big news in America, and here top names Gene Romero (3) and Pat Evans (51) fight for the best line on the corner during the annual classic at Ontario, California.

Right: Mecca for the road racer, the Isle of Man still has thrills and excitement. But the top men have refused to ride because of the dangerous nature of the course, and the event is losing its international importance.

locked away under ACU supervision. Nevertheless, Bob Dicker and Bert Mathers, with a potent inlet-over-exhaust Rudge outfit, did indeed fight their way through filthy weather in 1923 to set up a 24-hour sidecar record – even though the effort had to be spread over a five-day period.

But what of other countries? They, too, had their national *grands prix* meetings, but at first these were largely restricted to their own riders. However, British factories were on top in the racing world of the early '20s, and from about 1921 onward British works teams showed mounting interest in overseas meetings. Because they were the nearest to Britain, events like the Belgian and French *grands prix* were the first to attract attention from companies like Levis and New Imperial. On a two-stroke Levis, Geoff Davison underlined his

victory in the first 250 cc TT by winning the equivalent classes of the French and Belgian meetings. This, no doubt, encouraged British makers such as Norton and Sunbeam to spread their wings and include Continental meetings in their schedule.

It was valuable experience, because Continental manufacturers had been following their own line of development – rather more exotic, if slightly less successful. France, for instance, had a very advanced design in the 1924/6 500 cc Peugeot double-overhead-camshaft vertical twin; Italy, too, had very modern overhead-camshaft models by Bianchi and Moto-Guzzi, plus an interesting twin two-stroke from the Garelli works that had carried all before it in national competition. In Germany, DKW was pursuing the cause of the two-stroke, while BMW applied a policy of continual improvement to its transverse flat-twin.

For a while, Britain's singles (which, by the later 1920s, embraced single-overhead-camshaft models from Velocette, Norton and AJS) could more than hold their own. The first real fright for Britain came in 1926 when the Italians made an all-out effort to gain TT honours. Bianchi, Garelli and Moto-Guzzi invaded the Isle of Man, with Pietro Ghersi s 250 cc Moto-Guzzi as the most serious threat. Ghersi's pit-attendant was Carlo Guzzi himself, and practice had shown that the machine – a horizontal, overhead-camshaft single of traditional Guzzi design – was the quickest in the race. However, the makers had boobed in fitting too small a petrol tank, which meant that Ghersi would have to fill up no fewer than three times in the seven-lap event.

Britain's brightest hope was Paddy Johnston with his Blackburn-engined Cotton, and from the start the battle between this pair was on. Neither, however, had the best of luck. Ghersi took the lead, only to drop to second when he lost time fixing a loose carburettor. Johnston was bothered by a hand gear-change linkage. This disappeared completely on the last lap, leaving him to struggle over the mountain with the Cotton stuck in top gear. He made it, just about, with Ghersi coming home in what seemed to be second place, 20 seconds adrift. Uproar marred the prize-giving in Douglas that night, when the ACU officials announced that Pietro Ghersi had been excluded from the results on a technical foul. His entry form had stated that he was using a Lodge sparking plug but he had actually used an Italian-made Fert plug in the race, possibly for patriotic reasons.

A fundamental change in international racing took place in 1946, when the FIM banned supercharged models. And so the blown four-cylinder Gilera, victor of the 1939 Ulster Grand Prix, was already ancient history. So, too, was the blown, vertical-twin Velocette Roarer, given an outing during 1939 TT practising by Stanley Woods, but destined never to turn a wheel in earnest on a race circuit. AJS had been developing a supercharged twin with near-horizontal engine but, rather than scrap the design completely, decided to go

Previous pages: Barry Sheene, Kenny Roberts and Mick Grant – just three of the great names leaping away from the line at Brands Hatch to do battle over the Kent circuit on their superbikes – a breed of machine developed from participation in the American Daytona 200 meeting.

Top: Riders run for their machines at the start of the 24 hour Bol d'Or endurance race in France. Held over the Le Mans car-race circuit, the event features two riders per machine.

Above: One of Britain's most popular world champions, Phil Read has ridden for many different factories, including Yamaha and their great rivals MV Agusta in Italy. When Agostini left MV for Yamaha, Read became the number one on the red, four-cylinder Italian machines.

Right: With only minutes to go before the start of a 24 hour marathon, the bikes are lined up at the start of the Bol d'Or race at Le Mans. A full day later, very few will be left in at the finish.

ahead with conventional aspiration. The result was the Porcupine, so called from the spiky finning of the first examples.

With the coming of the 1950s, the privateer thus had a better selection of racing machinery from which to choose. Triumph offered the *Grand Prix* twin, based on the machine with which Ernie Lyons had won the 1946 Manx *Grand Prix*, first post-war race to make use of the time-honoured Isle of Man lap. From AJS came the 350 cc Model 7R (soon nicknamed the 'Boy Racer') which, in essence, constituted an updating of the pre-war R7 chain-driven overhead-camshaft model. Velocette's contribution was the Mk. VIII 350 cc with modern, hydraulically-damped rear suspension but, rather surprisingly, girder-type Webb front forks. For a while, production versions of the Manx Norton adhered to the plunger-type rear springing (the 'garden gate' frame) first tried out by the company in

the 1930s. But the works models had adopted the all-welded, duplex-tube frame designed by the McCandless brothers, and soon this, the Featherbed, was available to the buying public also.

Such, then, were the tools with which the new generation of riders were to learn their trade. They were sturdy, relatively simple machines, which meant that repairs and adjustments could be carried out in an open and congested paddock, and they possessed a reasonable turn of speed.

The Norton, AJS and Velocette were production racers, not production-machine racers. The difference is a vital one, as we shall see if we study the rise of the BSA Gold Star. First, the name. In pre-war days it had been the habit of the British Motor Cycle Racing Club to award a gold star (in actuality a little enamelled star bearing the numerals '100', to be attached to the club lapel badge) to any rider topping 161 km/h (100 mph) in any Brooklands meeting organized by the club. The BSA works hit on the idea of bringing the illustrious Wal Handley out of retirement to ride a works-tuned 500 cc BSA Empire Star (running on alcohol) in a Bemsee meeting. The plot worked, Wal got his gold star, and BSA forthwith marketed a 'Gold Star' model derived from the Handley racer. The machine was revived, in both 350 and 500 cc versions, in the post-war BSA programme.

Now, for the 1947 TT programme, the organizing ACU thought up the Junior and Senior Clubman's TT races, the machines for which would have to be catalogued roadsters – though lighting sets and silencers could be removed in the interests of safety. This, therefore, was production-machine racing, and although the field for the initial races of the series included a mixture of Norton Internationals, Royal Enfield Bullets, Triumph Tiger 100s, and Ariel Red Hunters, the one machine that grew to dominate the scene was the BSA Gold Star. By 1955 the domination was virtually complete, with 33 of the 37 starters in the 1955 Junior Clubman's race mounted on Goldies.

Trouble was, the Goldie was that little bit too good, and thereby virtually signed its own death warrant. Clubman racing was dropped from the TT programme, and it was left to Thruxton to continue waving the production-machine racing flag, with the marathon race known at first as the Thruxton Nine-Hour, and later as the 500 Miler.

As surfaces broke up, or the venues were turned over to other purposes, airfield and army camp racing began to take a back seat. Silverstone survived, because the track had been aquired by the British Racing Drivers' Club, but only the occasional motorcycle meeting was held there. However, all was far from lost, for new circuits were coming into use. In Kent, Brands Hatch had long been the venue for big-scale grass-track meetings, as also had Mallory Park, near Leicester; indeed, team racing between Mallory Park and Brands Hatch grass-trackers had been quite a feature of the early 1950s. Now both venues were given a tarmac coating, to re-emerge as short road-race circuits. In Cheshire, the internal roads of a country estate known as Oulton Park were joined up and tarred to form yet another new race track.

So the machines, and the venues, were now at hand, and from this forcing bed emerged the stars-to-be – Bob McIntyre, Derek Minter, Percy Tait, Phil Read and so many more. And Geoff Duke? Ah, now that is another story. Geoff was never a member of the short-circuit scratchers. Instead, when war ended he was a corporal instructor in the Royal Signals, and he became one of the first members of the post-war Royal Signals Display Team. On demobilization he joined BSA as a trials rider, and from there, still with trials-riding as the objective, he transferred to the Norton factory. A win, on a Norton, in the 1949 Senior Clubman's TT showed that he could travel quickly, as well as precisely, and a switch to the official Norton race team was inevitable.

By the mid 1950s the challenge to Britain from abroad was only too obvious, with Italy leading the attack. Italians mainly contested the smaller classes, with Mondial, Moto Morini tackling the 125 cc races and Moto Guzzi aiming at the 250 cc stuff. But that was far from all. Back had come the four-cylinder Gilera, soon to be partnered by the similar MV Agusta four. And Germany could certainly not be ruled out with its potent little 125 and 250 cc NSUs, the first racing motorcycles to adopt a dolphin-type streamlined fairing (of hand-beaten sheet aluminium, in this instance).

The total eclipse of the British racing effort came in 1956, when every solo TT class was won by an Italian machine. But three years later there was yet another change. From Japan, to compete in the 1959 125 cc TT, arrived a trio of smart little twins, watchlike in the delicacy of their construction, but outclassed in speed. Next year,

Honda was back again, with some even more complex pieces of machinery: four-cylinder 250s, with no fewer than 16 valves apiece. Another Japanese outfit had come along, too, with some very ordinary-seeming two-stroke twins. The name was Suzuki.

Yet if Britain's machinery was outclassed, its riders certainly were not, and, ironically, it was with British pilots that the foreign challengers were to climb to ever greater glory. Geoff Duke, followed by Bob McIntyre, moved to the Gilera camp. John Surtees, and later Mike Hailwood, went to MV Agusta. Sammy Miller switched from Mondial to CZ. And when yet another Japanese make appeared on the scene, Bill Ivy was the man who brought Yamaha initial success.

Through the between-war years, America had turned its back on motorcycles, with only Indian and Harley-Davidson as survivors of a once-thriving native industry. From the 1950s onward, however, a considerable sporting market had grown there, and America had become a customer well worth wooing. Major sporting occasion on the USA calendar was the Daytona 200, initially a somewhat peculiar event staged partly on the beach, and incorporating huge bends of banked-up sand. That image was to change with the building of a new stadium featuring an odd compromise between a concrete speed saucer and a twisty, flat infield. Over the years evolved a formula for a racing machine, nominally at least, derived from a roadster model. Machines built for British-style production-model racing just wouldn't do. Factories such as BSA-Triumph, to whom the American market was of vital importance, therefore had to build semi-roadster racers to two different standards.

Only in recent years has the Isle of Man TT fallen into line by

Above: Sidecars may be slower than solos but, for thrills and action, they are out on their own. For years the German-built BMW twins were unbeatable, but now a host of specials have pushed the Munich marvels from top spot.

Top right: Road racing is now big business with many firms, from oil companies to finance houses, helping to sponsor riders. In return, they cover their machines with the symbols of their helpers, as in this shot of John Newbold on a 500 cc Suzuki in Finland.

Right: There are more cameramen than riders, but it is the racers the crowds came to watch. Soon this pack of starters in the 1976 Austrian 500 cc world championship event will be fighting it out for the victor's honours.

adopting Formula 750 racing. Meanwhile, the British public had been given a glimpse of the flamboyant American racing men with the introduction of the Easter-time team races between British and USA riders, held at the Brands Hatch, Mallory Park and Oulton Park circuits. First this series was a BSA-Triumph promotion, with the riders from both countries mounted on machines of one or other make, but it has now become Formula 750, and the machines are Kawasakis, Yamahas and Suzukis.

Sadly, the Isle of Man TT has declined in importance as a factor in the world road-racing championships. By 1977, the meeting no longer counted as a championship round in the traditional sense, although it conceivably stood on the threshold of a new and exciting career, as the first of the genuine road-racing championships. The mantle of the British Grand Prix has shifted to the ACU-organized Silverstone International. Nevertheless, Silverstone will never rival the charisma of the Isle of Man, nor can it ever replace the mountainous island as a testing ground for frame, suspension, or transmission developments.

ENDUROS &ISDT

ROYALENFIELDKAWASAKIBULTACOVELOCETTE HONDAJAMESBMWTRIUMPHDUCATISUZUKIH

INDIANJAWAMVAUGUSTACZHENDERSONMONTESAMATCHLESS

YAMAHAHUSQVARNANORTON

Enduro and ISDT riding
in multi-day, marathon events
have bred a unique style
of man and machine,
each capable of flat-out
performance for hour after
hour, day after day,
over ground so rough
that other, lesser mortals
would be looking for
a detour.

Every sport has its heroes and motorcycling is no exception. No branch of two-wheel motorcycling could have been devised that is more likely to produce deeds of valour than the International Six Days' Trial. A 3,200 km (2,000 mile) near race over the roughest imaginable territory, riding for one's country on machines allowed little or no servicing must produce its heroes, and every year the International Six Days' Trial does just that.

The trial kicked off in the dark days of 1913, just before World War I, when France sent a team of three men to compete against Britain in the already established ACU Six-Day Reliability Trial. The idea behind the event was to demonstrate the viability of the motorcycle as a reliable means of transport, and the machines used were built from standard production models. The plan was to improve the breed and that the ISDT had done ever since. The rules for that original contest included loss of marks for using spares to stay mobile and for failing to climb certain designated hills. Britain won convincingly.

The following year, though, it was France's turn to play host, and the French mapped out a course centred at Grenoble and featuring many long-drawn-out hills that the French hoped would show the superiority of their home-built machines over the British mounts. But the event was never held. At the last moment, after the British machines had been shipped to France, the international situation deteriorated to the extent that the event was called off.

Six years later, in 1920, the French ran their event at Grenoble and their adversaries were Swiss not British (British factories had decided to boycott the event following a row over another French trial earlier in the year). The Swiss trio confounded all the pundits and came out on top. For the following year, 1921, the Swiss ran the event, establishing a tradition that the winning country would have the option of staging the following year's contest.

For 1921, only Britain officially challenged and again the Swiss won, underlining their superiority 12 months later by beating Britain and Sweden for the international trophy. Swedes came out winners in 1923 for their sole victory in the history of the event. But British manufacturers had begun to see the value of the competition in establishing world outlets for their products, and for 1924 spent what were then vast sums preparing their machines – to such effect that the British monopolized the event for the next six years. Italy scored its only successes in 1930 and 1931.

From then on the event known as the 'olympics of motorcycling' took on political overtones. The Nazi Party was determined to prove the superior technology of German industry. The Germans demonstrated their skills for the three years from 1932 to 1934, fielding the most powerful machines seen in ISDT history. British manufacturers got together and produced machines that equalled the German hat trick during the following three years. In 1938 the top development engineers of each country set out to produce machines to compete in the following year's event, not knowing that this would end in chaos.

More than 100 British riders (by far the largest foreign contingent) travelled to Salzburg, then part of the German Reich, to compete against the crack, government-backed German and Italian line-ups. What greeted them were vast armies of swastika-wearing officials lining the routes and, although the trial started as scheduled, it was clear that it would be a race to get the meeting finished before hostilities began. After two days the French contingent pulled out and rushed for the border. Eager to avert the event's entire collapse, German officials guaranteed British riders a problem-free exit from Germany after the trial. But on the fourth evening a telegram arrived from the British consul-general in Berlin warning British subjects to leave Germany without delay. British factories, hearing the grave news, ordered their teams home, and although the British Army riders stayed for another day, they too, then fled – two days before the meeting's scheduled end. The trial ground to a finish with Germany and Italy inevitably taking the awards. Later, though, the *Fédération Internationale Motocycliste* declared that these unrepresentative results should be struck from record books.

After a gap of seven years, Czechoslovakia took over the organization and made a clean sweep of the results, winning the Trophy Award for the team mounted on bikes made within the entering country and also the Vase for riders permitted to compete on foreign-made mounts. The following six years became a struggle between Czechoslovakia and Britain with the British teams winning five times, but always harassed by the Czechs.

After winning in 1953, Britain completely faded from the ISDT picture and West Germany emerged to battle it out with Czechoslovakia for the premier Trophy Award. Again politics came into the sport as East Germany created a massive ISDT team of pseudo-army riders – nominally members of the armed forces, but virtually professional riders whose entire time was devoted to training for the event. In 1963 MZ machines of East Germany took the Trophy and they managed it for the next four years as well. In 1968 West Germany nosed in for a solitary win, but MZ made it again in 1969. During the preceding few years the Jawa company of Czechoslovakia had been developing a new two-stroke design, and its plans came to

Previous pages: Mud, confusion and riders going all ways – that is what enduro riding can be all about. For riders not only have to get from A to B as quickly as possible – they have to contend with conditions like this, and worse, on the way.

Above: Two of the all-time enduro greats. Czechs Zenek Cespiva and Josef Cisar work frantically on their battered Jawa machines in an effort to get them ready for another day's punishment during an International Six Days Trial.

Top right: The only ISDT yet to be held in America was the 1972 event where, although Czechoslovakia again took the major Trophy award, the home team won the secondary Vase prize on Penton machines. A major fire on a machine on the opening day lost them any chance of the Trophy.

Right: Although competitors in ISDTs and enduros normally start at one-minute intervals, the action really begins when the faster men try to pass slower rivals who have started in front of them.

fruition in 1970 when the Czechs started a fantastic five-year success story, winning the Trophy each year and only missing out on the Vase once. And it was that failure in the Vase that gave America its best placing in the contest.

For years American attempts at the ISDT had been amateurish efforts. But in the 1970s the Penton factory began an association with the event that culminated in its Vase win at the Dalton, Massachusetts, venue in 1973 – the first time the meeting had been held in the United States. Then West Germany took command of the situation, winning the Golden Jubilee event in 1975 in the Isle of Man and seizing the premier award again a year later in Austria.

What makes the ISDT unique is its combination of a 3,200 km (2,000 mile) scramble and a reliability run. Riders are required to achieve set speeds over various sections of the countryside. Penalty

marks acquired through lateness are added to performances in a series of moto-cross special tests and a hard-surface road-race test at the finish of the event. Machines evolved for the ISDT are basically reliable scramblers with the accent on ease of maintenance. The rules are very strict, though, on just what mechanical work may be done. Before the event, each machine is taken into a special scrutineering bay where officials attach special paint and marking wire to those parts that should remain unchanged for the duration of the trial. The fact that many of the parts *are* altered surreptitiously is widely regarded more as a tribute to the ingenuity of the team managers than as a sign of perfidy. 'If you're caught you're out, but if you get away with it, well and good,' seems to be the general attitude. Indeed, more stigma is attached to getting caught than to the act of cheating. One team manager who had given his services to the event for many years arranged a double-bike swap – completely changing the machines of two of his competitors during the event. The ploy was discovered at the final day's check. Although the fiddle was hushed up by the international jury who meet to discuss any rule-bending, the local federation summarily dismissed the team manager from his post for the next year's event. Had the ploy worked he would have no doubt been treated as a hero.

Risks run by riders in the ISTD are high. At near flat-out speeds, they must contend not only with unknown territory but sometimes with on-coming traffic. For the event is usually held over tracks and paths, and in the depths of rural regions not every peasant expects a sudden confrontation with a rider scratching hard to stay on time for his country. The achievements of some riders against near-impossible odds would make great adventure fiction, were they not true. To ride the ISDT distance in just six days requires superb physical fitness and tremendous skill. But that's not all. The man must have a deep-seated, almost uncanny feeling for the machinery that carries him. And, if something goes wrong with the mechanism,

he needs the ability of a highly skilled fitter in order to repair it fast.

The average rider may take an hour mending a rear-tyre puncture, given air line, warmth, good lights and other workshop facilities. To stand any hope of making ·a national team, a seasoned ISDT campaigner must be able to stop, remove his wheel, take off the tyre, replace the inner tube, inflate by hand pump or air bottle, replace the wheel and ride away – all in under four minutes. He will be ready to tear down fences for wire to hold ·a broken frame together, know how to make splints out of two tyre levers for a fractured swinging arm, and may be continually chewing gum with which to plug a leaking fuel tank if the need arises.

And if the machines take punishment, so, too, do the riders. To them, broken fingers are just a nuisance, smashed toes a mere difficulty. Every team worth its salt has its own physician ready at the checkpoints to give copious quantities of pain-killing drugs just to keep the riders on the move.

The ISDT is the greatest of all enduros, but its days may well be numbered, for it's an event where accidents are commonplace and vast areas of land are necessary. Within very few years the meeting may give way to a series of shorter trials held in various countries. Already such events are taking place and there has been a European two-day championship for many years. These contests are simply mini-ISDTs, with up to 200 riders following a route marked either with cards or by dye, and again aiming to get to each checkpoint along the course inside the time limit.

The idea of the European championship was put forward by West German Otto Sensburg, a former competitor in the ISDT. Sensburg worked on the theory that organizers would have an easier time running events of only two days' duration and that manufacturers would be more likely to compete, as he envisaged a series of winners at each trial – one for each capacity class. As it turned out, the contest became a private war between Czechoslovakia on Jawa machines in the larger-capacity classes, and the West German Zundapps in the up-to-175 cc categories.

Enduros and off-road riding in America have become a big national sport, with some states setting aside vast tracts of land for the motor-cyclist for whom the tarmac is too tame. Enormous, commercially run parks have also opened up. These not only give the benefit of scenic trail rides for their customers but the advantages of nearby medical help in case of accident, and a get-you-home service in the event of machine failure.

The majority of machines currently being sold as enduro racers or trail bikes are very far from that. Just as the world enjoyed a scooter vogue in the 1950s, the 1970s have seen a fashion for so-called off-road machines. The majority of these are compromise bikes, being purely sports roadsters with a few off-road adjuncts such as high-level mudguards, high-rise handle-bars and sports-model tyres. Such machines are much more at home on the road but do offer the adventurous rider a chance to explore green lanes, forest tracks and even deserts.

Desert racing is a speciality of the Americans who possess the vast wasteland areas of the type needed for this sport. If anything, desert racing is more of a long-distance scramble than the enduro or the ISDT. Here, there are no speed schedules: it is simply the quickest man to the finish who gets the laurels. Such events are often held with riders leaving at one-minute intervals, although some start with a line of competitors stretching almost 1.6 km (1 mile) across the desert waiting for a mass-start signal from a smoke rocket in the distance. It is from such desert riders that America is hoping to breed its new ISDT heroes.

Top left: The line stretches as far as the eye can see. No flag will start this American desert enduro – instead, a maroon will be fired, and then the whole pack will be off to the first check point, an hour's racing away.

Left: The beauty of the Berkshire Hills in Massachusetts echoes to the sound of a dirt bike as an American competitor in the 1972 International Six Days Trial makes up time on some of the easiest sections of the 1,600 kilometre (1,000 mile) route.

Right: Desert riding is big news in California. Although a super-modern dirt bike is necessary to get up in the awards, many riders have fun on much cheaper machines, such as this old Triumph.

MOTO CROSS

It's the fastest growing spectator sport in the motorcycle calendar – and no wonder, for moto-cross attracts the new iron men on two and three wheels. Closed, short-circuit races over tortuous circuits have enthusiasts packing the ropes to cheer their national heroes to the chequered flag.

The number-one national sport in many European countries is fast on the increase. In fact moto-cross – cross-country racing over a short circuit – has been around since the birth of motorcycling. And although today racers are riding faster, fiercer machines with much more at stake, they have nothing on the adventurous pioneers of moto-cross who rode their heavy touring machines to the circuit, stripped off excess weight such as lights, mudguards and silencers, and got set to do battle in the countryside. With virtually no rear suspension and very little at the front, riders bumped and humped their way over heathland circuits. Such meetings had something of the enduro about them, for a lap could be all of 50 kilometres (30 miles) long and riders were required to cover the circuit once in the morning and, after a gentlemanly stop for lunch, again in the afternoon.

The name 'moto-cross' comes from the French, who coined it simply for cross-country motorcycle racing, and it was in France and Belgium that the sport first boomed. The Continentals brought to the public the spectacle of tight racing over short courses. Already, by the early 1950s, crowds of up to 60,000 were common at such events and, as the public paid to watch, so the prize money available to riders multiplied. This in turn meant that factories gained publicity and could spend more on developing super-specialized machines to deal with the tortuous tracks. Power for a given engine size has gone up and up. But pure power itself cannot win scrambles, for to drive the rear wheel along the road the tyre must be kept in contact with the dirt, and to this end much work has been done to improve suspension, and many of the improvements learned on the moto-cross circuits have been incorporated into road-going designs.

The British Matchless firm contributed much with its telescopic front fork shortly after World War II. Norton soon bettered this advance, but it was not until the Italian Cerani company came into the business with precision-made components allowing a full 15 cm (6 inches) of movement that people appreciated just what improved suspension could add to performance. Rear suspension, too, has moved up – from plunger rear frames, to swinging arms with oil and spring suspension units, and now to today's sophisticated gas-damped systems and complex parallel linkages.

Back in the 1950s with the two-leg moto-cross system just gaining ground, the fields were dominated by big 500 cc single-cylinder machines. Works-sponsored riders rode BSA, Matchless, Norton and AJS bikes, also similar machines from Husqvarna in Sweden and FN in Belgium. Eventually these bikes were producing phenomenal horsepower figures, but their overall weight of around 140 kg (300 lb) limited just how much power could be used.

Today's factory machine weighs around 80 kg (180 lb), less than two-thirds that of the big four-stroke singles, and the machines would be lighter still were it not for international regulations governing their weight on grounds of safety. The small, lightweight two-stroke that now dominates racing in all but the sidecar class started showing its muscles in the 250 cc category and probably saved the quarter-litre class from extinction. Back in the early 1960s, 250 cc scrambling had been pretty dull to watch. Bikes were under-powered and overweight and it wasn't until high-performance two-stroke engines began to be developed by such firms as Husqvarna, Greeves and CZ that the class came into its own. Riders who had tried the smaller-capacity bikes and found their handling infinitely superior to large-cc machines soon started entering the little 250s in the 500 cc races – and winning too. Organizers quickly put a halt to this by limiting the 500 cc events to machines of between 350 and 500 cc, but this didn't stop the two-strokes. Factories simply uprated their 250 cc machines to above the lower limit and today's *Grand Prix* championship machines are usually between 360 and 400 cc. True, the factories could enlarge them to the full 500 cc, but they believe their present engines develop sufficient power – in fact more power than the track enables them to use.

The new breed of lightweight two-strokes brought in a hoard of amateur riders from Europe and America, all keen to start racing on machines that did not demand the strength of a Mr. Universe, and could be expected to perform week after week without major overhaul.

Previous pages: The style that makes a champion. Swiss Robert Grogg and passenger Andies Graber power-slide their 750 cc Norton Wasp machine to Victory in a 1975 European Sidecar Championship race. Now Japanese engines are taking over from the big British twins.

Above: International moto-cross is no place to worry about getting dirty, as Dutch ace Jak Velthoven shows. He is used to getting dirty, for racing goes on all year round – whatever the weather.

Right: Reckoned by many experts to be the best of the new breed of American moto-cross riders, Brad Lackey spends the summer months touring the world Grand Prix circuits in a bid to pick up points for the world title.

And it was when the youth of America started going moto-cross mad that the Japanese saw the market and moved in, buying the best riders and, without doubt, producing the best machines.

Suzuki went the whole hog with this, eventually employing world champions Joel Robert and Roger de Coster, and sitting them on the most expensive machinery ever produced. Suzuki's no-expense-spared policy included using exotic materials like titanium in the frames, and at one stage the firm had the weight of its *Grand Prix* bikes down to just over 70 kg (160 lb). With this type of machine Suzuki won the world 250 cc title at its first attempt, and held on for a further two years with Joel Robert at the helm. But what a price was paid. Each machine bore an enormous cost and lasted only five or six meetings before rapid wear of the ultra-light components reduced the bike to scrap. However, just to prove its 250 cc title was no fluke, Suzuki switched to the 500 cc class, hired its second Belgian – Roger de Coster – and achieved exactly the same results.

Although such factories still employ the top riders at movie-star salaries, spending on machines has been brought down to a saner limit. Instead of curbing cash outlay, the *FIM* accomplished this reduction by imposing a minimum weight limit that made the use of ultra-light and expensive materials of no advantage. This put most factories on a level footing, and as the major companies already

get sufficient power from their highly tuned engines, development now focusses upon improving the transfer of engine thrust to the rear wheel and thence to the road. A moto-cross machine spends much time in the air, flying over bumps and jumps. But while its rear wheel is airborne the machine cannot be driven forward. Current suspension technology is thus aimed less at giving the rider an easier time than at keeping the rear wheel on the ground as long as possible to keep the engine usefully employed.

What all the factories are after is the World Championship. There are four championship classes: 125 cc, 250 cc and 500 cc solo and a special 1,000 cc sidecar class. Before the start of each season, top riders nominate the class in which they will compete that year. They can then score points only in that category.

The world-championship rounds run to over 40 events held all around the globe, but that just isn't enough for the moto-cross-hungry spectators, and a whole series of smaller events has sprouted, including a 12-race trans-AMA series in America and also major multi-round events in Australia and New Zealand.

Because of the large sums paid by top factories for world-class riders and the numbers of championship series held throughout the world, a host of riders are now full-time professionals. And many are earning very good money indeed. People of the calibre of De Coster are national heroes and spend their mid-week days touring local circuits to give demonstrations before each circuit holds its next home derby. Mid-week events are not unusual on the Continent, even in the winter months, for, as with soccer, floodlights can banish darkness.

If solo riders are full-time professionals earning big sums with factory contracts, the same is certainly not true of the sidecar brigade. As very few companies produce machines for sidecar work, most have little interest in championship series, and the men who ride the title rounds are usually sponsored by large dealers. Sidecar scrambling was a very hit-or-miss affair until the 1960s. The favourite machine was a Tribsa, a combination of Triumph engine and BSA frame, but it was heavy and unwieldly, and only when the small English firm of Wasp began making a series of purpose-built bike frames combined with sidecar chassis did the sport get truly off the ground. Wasp held sway for many years, but other manufacturers, copying the idea of an integral frame, have now leapt on the band wagon.

For sidecar use the Triumph-Bonneville engine eventually gave way to the Norton Twin when Norton produced an 850 cc version of its famous Dominator power unit. Although this is still going with a measure of success, more exotic power plants like those from Yamaha, Honda and Kawasaki are edging the Norton from the top spot.

Even the Russians have tried their hand at world-class sidecar moto-cross, with designs based on their Cossack Ural horizontally opposed 650 cc twin. But, as the design is basically that of a 20-year-old BMW, the amount of power that can be obtained reliably for two 30-minute races is limited, and only the sheer strength of the Russian riders – who seem to speed up toward the end of an event as other European contenders start flagging – has brought them any degree of success.

Moto-cross is booming now in many nations, including the late-starter America which, back in the early 1970s, had the distinction of having Jim Pomeroy win the first *Grand Prix* for the United States.

Previous pages: It's fast and furious with very little margin for error. At the first corner of a crowded race, such as this in America, there is no question of looking for the best line – you just go along with the mob.

Left: It is a long way down for American Gary Semics during the 1975 United States 500 cc Grand Prix, but he made it safely to the bottom. Semics rides Kawasaki, but the big class in world moto-cross has been dominated by Suzuki, giving no other manufacturers much of a look in.

Top right: Natural circuits, many of them carved out of disused gravel pits, not only provide the riders with testing conditions but give made-to-measure grandstand facilities for the crowds.

Right: They went thataway! A following rider, particularly in a sidecar race, has to contend with flying mud when conditions are wet, or a sea of dust, clogging the eyes and parching the throat, in dry weather.

AT THE DRAGS

Drag racing is the one branch of
motorcycle sport where
the rider takes second place to
his machine. The machines used
are the wildest, starkest
and most powerful in the game.
They are built to accelerate –
and that means 290 kilometres
per hour (180 mph) in around eight
seconds from a
standing start.

Just try this experiment. Count up to eight seconds. By the time you finish, a drag bike unleashed the moment you began could be 400 metres (a quarter of a mile) away and travelling at around 300 km/h (190 mph). For the fact is that the most powerful motorcycle engines ever produced are not in exotic road-racers at Daytona, nor are they in the mighty scrambles machines – they are at the drags. Drag racing is the one branch of motorcycle sport where virtually anything goes. And anything means just that: any size of engine, any number of engines, any fuel, any supercharger. And these way-out creations, among the most expensive machines ever built, are simply designed to run for around nine seconds and to cover just 400 metres (a quarter of a mile) per outing.

Drag racing, or sprinting as it was then known, originated in Britain in the 1920s when competitors took turns to try to beat the clock over a measured 400 m (quarter-mile). But a greater sense of competition, or maybe better facilities, made the USA the effective inventor of simultaneous competition: two riders taking off at the same time to add zest to the performance.

It all sounds very simple. The rider just sits on his machine and, at a given signal, accelerates until he crosses a marked line 400 m (quarter of a mile) away. The individual with the shortest time is the winner. But this is a race that can be won by a hundredth of a second, and the machines developed for it are wild in the extreme.

In the 1950s, when the sport began blooming in Britain and America, a favourite tuning technique was simply to reduce weight. All possible extras were stripped from the machines, and many models took on the semblance of honeycomb as riders drilled copious holes to leave only the structurally vital minimum in materials. But the real first speed breakthrough came with the adoption of special fuels. Methanol was the first and commonest form of fuel used for drag cycles. Its great advantage was that it held more oxygen than petrol and would therefore burn more fiercely, adding to the power of the engine. Its snags were that the machine could be more difficult to start and had to be run very richly to avoid risk of seizures. Americans invented a simple starting technique to overcome the first problem, placing the rear wheel on rollers spun by the rear wheels of a car or truck.

After methanol, which added power, came nitro methane, which multiplied it. Once nitro blends were mixed with methanol, power increased like December sales of Christmas cards, and riders found they were actually developing far more than their rear wheels could transmit to the tarmac. On getting the signal to go, a rider would open the throttle, drop the clutch and the rear wheel would simply spin in a cloud of blue smoke. What was needed to solve this problem was a wide flat tyre without tread patterns, so that the largest possible amount of rubber could be in contact with the road. Riders knew this was the answer because, for many years, such tyres had worked on large drag-racing cars in America. The British Avon company was first in the field with a 10 cm (4 inch) wide tyre which it christened 'The Slick' because of its treadless pattern. This boosted performance considerably, but the added traction of the rear was providing problems of its own. If the rear tyre gripped instead of spun, the front wheel of the machine could rear up uncontrollably. To counter this, makers built long, low special frames, and each rider lay nearly prone across the top of the power plant.

With wheel bases lengthened, power-hungry riders soon spotted that the gap between the engine and the front wheel was big enough to take another power plant. This they soon added, and double-engined Nortons, Triumphs, BSAs, Harley-Davidsons and Hondas are now common sights on the drag strips of Europe and America. But development did not stop there. The American M & H company produced even wider slicks giving yet better traction. Again the search for power was on, this time leading to a third engine and to twin power plants of unheard-of sizes.

The first under-10-second run was accomplished by former speedway ace Alf Hagon with the aid of a supercharged and super-tuned 1,300 cc JAP engine. The bike developed sufficient power to operate on only one gear, but this was enough to drive it at 260 km/h (160 mph) from

Previous pages: To increase the traction of the rear tyre, drag racers like to warm it up a little, prior to a run – and what better way than with a little fire? But there's no danger, because before the flames can do anything but warm the tyre, the bike and rider are long gone.

Above: That's an awful lot of engine. And it is more than it looks, for each of these three four-cylinder Honda engines has been opened up from its original 750 cc to a staggering 1,000 cc.

Top right: The same bike in action with rider Russ Collins doing his best to stretch his frame over all 12 cylinders of his machine, which reaches about 290 kilometres per hour (180 mph) from a standing start in just 400 metres (¼ mile).

Right: With two 1,300 cc vee-twin Harley-Davidson engines burning a potent brew of nitro-methane and methanol, it is no wonder that the rear tyre, although wide, cannot cope with the power.

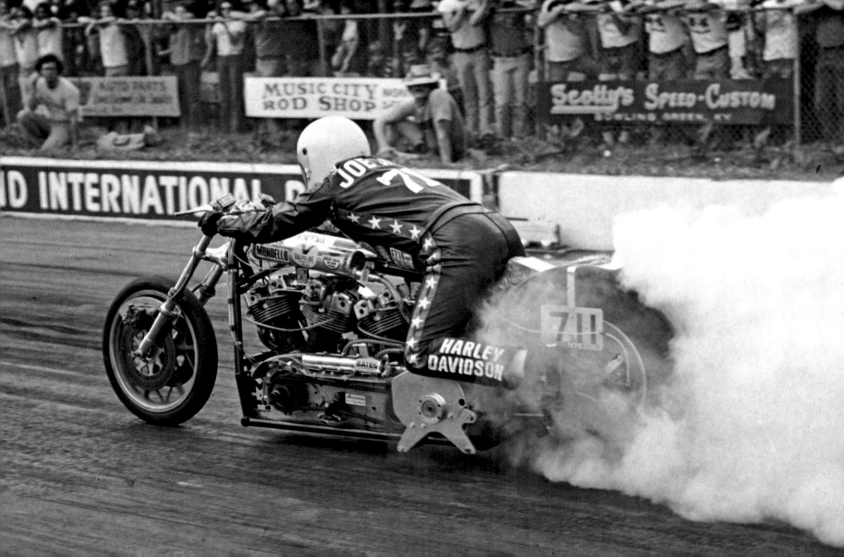

Above: England is fast catching up with her more speedy transatlantic enthusiasts. Using many American ideas, Ray Feltell achieves fantastic performances with a single-engined 650 cc Triumph.

Right: For years the fastest man in the world over the standing-start quarter mile, American Tom Christensen achieves success using a highly tuned pair of British-made Norton twins fitted into a one-off frame with special slider clutch.

standstill. Hagon's technique was simple. He would sit at the line, rev the engine to near bursting point and just drop the clutch. Even with its Avon slick the rear tyre spun, and continued spinning the entire length of the straight. For some years this technique remained the norm, but it was a hit-or-miss affair, and the road surface of the drag strip was over-important to the rider's performance. Using just one gear had an obvious advantage, however, for it meant that no time was lost in changing up. Progress now came from America with a very special clutch that would slip at the start, allowing full engine revs without rear-wheel spin, and then slowly grip as the bike tore up the short drag strip. With these aids machines were soon turning in performances of under eight seconds and a seven-second run became only a matter of time.

The Americans predominate in the field of drag racing, much of their success deriving from their numerous special strips with surfaces designed to provide maximum grip.

STUNT RIDING

The stunt riders of the
motorcycle world – whether
they are crashing through
plate glass, negotiating burning
tunnels, leaping buses
or attempting to wheelie the
length of the TT circuit –
are the circus kings of the sport.
Their job is entertainment,
and that's what they deliver,
just as does the high-wire act
under the big top.

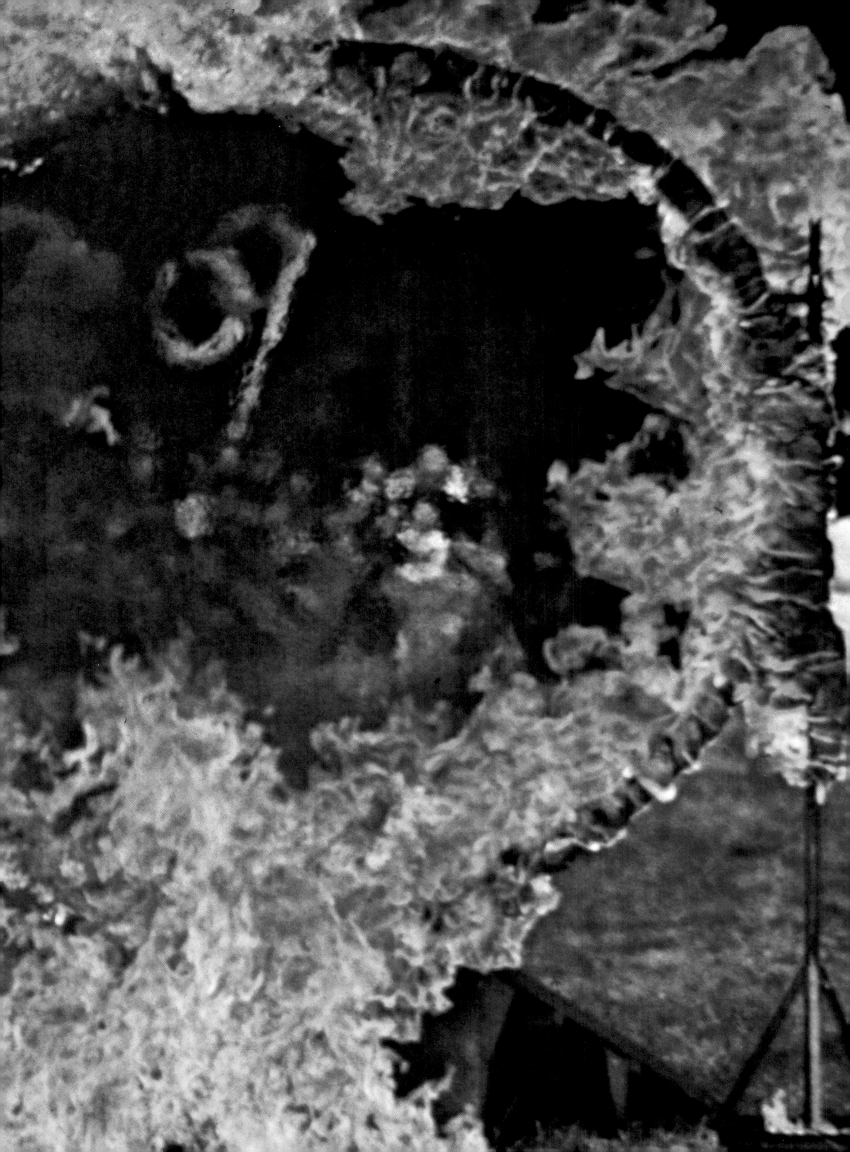

'I don't mind if you take me to the hospital after my stunt as long as you go via the bank'. Those much-quoted words from Evel Knievel sum up the simple philosophy behind the current vogue of stunt riding as represented by its uncrowned king. Knievel is a professional. He rides stunts for hard cash, and, if he's not a millionaire already, he is well on target. Knievel has a shrewd business brain lodged in his accident-scarred, limping body. He remembers each broken bone and abrasion not for a jump mis-judged but for another addition to his bank account. And he deserves every penny he makes. For, although Evel was not the first of the stunt men, he was the first to make motorcycle jumping big business and brought to it a degree of showmanship that has made his name a household word.

Knievel's repertoire is, in fact, fairly limited. He will line up a given number of buses, trucks or cars, have ramps built at each end of the line, then, after some tension-building false starts, launch his machine over them. Critics can dispute the actual number of vehicles leapt for it's true that the take-off ramp extends over the first two or three and the landing ramp does the same thing the other end. But the Knievel act is a pure piece of showmanship and no one that has seen it has gone away dissatisfied.

That was until the Snake River disaster. For five years before the actual attempt Knievel had been talking to the press about his plans to jump a rocket-assisted motorcycle over the Grand Canyon. It didn't quite work out that way. The Grand Canyon bid was put off for a variety of reasons, and the eventual attempt took place at the much less impressive Snake River Canyon. And, far from being a rocket-assisted motorcycle, Knievel's projectile was just about pure rocket. With the crowd gathered, admission money received, television rights arranged and the blue touch paper finally lit, all that the spectators and viewers saw was a rocket soar a short distance into the air and then come down by parachute. The Snake River stunt did the cause of show riding no good at all. It suffered further from the rash of Knievel imitators that broke out on both sides of the Atlantic. One man has a died a horrible death in a tunnel of blazing straw attempting a so-called world record, and even young schoolboys are now forming groups for so-called stunt-riding displays.

But there are still real stunt riders, and very exciting their performances can be. Knievel jumping his buses puts on a tremendous show. But so, too, do more mundane but equally skilful riders such as the members of the English Metropolitan Police and Royal Marines display teams who weekly excite crowds with balancing feats and pyramid building on moving machines at charity shows throughout the country. They may substitute precision for sheer danger but their shows are enjoyment none the less.

Among the latest recruits to the growing army of stunt riders is Englishman Dave Taylor who must be the wheelie king to end them all. Taylor's speciality is riding a motorcycle, supported only by its back wheel, for mile after mile. In 1976 he enlivened crowds gathered for the Tourist Trophy in the Isle of Man by attempting the complete circuit of more than 59 km (37 mile) on the rear wheel of a Yamaha model. True, he had to drop the front wheel to the ground once or twice, but many spectators rated his effort more exciting than the actual racing that followed.

The growing popularity of motorcycles has also seen a growth of stunt-riding episodes in a glut of chase movies. This tradition probably started with George Formby's *No Limit* comedy film about the TT in which some spectacular stunt riding was performed by the stars of the '30s. It continued with titles like *The Great Escape*, where Steve McQueen was seen escaping from a German prison camp by leaping his motorcycle over the barbed-wire fence. The fact that our hero had a stand-in – Australian Tim Gibbes – to do the trick didn't detract from the movie one iota.

Stunt riding is now part and parcel of the motocycle scene. Spectators at American short-track events can expect displays during the intervals and the same thing is happening at speedway meetings and at road-racing circuits all over the motorcycling world.

Previous pages: It is not as dangerous as it looks, but then stunt riding is to provide thrills, and the well-known hoop of fire does just that. For years the blazing hoop of straw has been the high spot of many displays.

Above: Evel Knievel does it again as he takes a flying leap over a row of trucks. It is with such feats that he has made himself America's, and possibly the world's, no. 1 motorcycle stunt rider.

Right: Dave Taylor, Great Britain's answer to Knievel, displays his speciality – rearing and riding a motorcycle on its back wheels.

CUSTOM BIKES

Bike manufacturers spend
fortunes on giant design teams
attempting to produce a
machine to attract the shoppers.
But, for some enthusiasts,
all this is not enough.
A customizing ace can take a
stock machine, cut it,
re-vamp the frame and produce
a glorious technicolour
paint job that speaks just one
word – individuality.

Virtually banned in some countries, idolized in others, the current chopper craze can easily be summed up in the one phrase – you like 'em or you hate 'em. The chopper theoretically represents one man's idea of extending his personality to the machine he rides. The chopper cult was born in California, which is still its home. The personalized motorcycle that comes from America's West Coast may be way out, may be freaky, may even be functionally alarming, but many choppers are works of art.

A chopper freak isn't really interested in performance. He can't be interested in comfort. He's just interested in being seen on a machine that is so extraordinary that every head turns at its approach.

The basic chopper lacks rear suspension, has front forks up to about 45 cm (18 in) longer than standard, a mini front wheel and foot rests set high and forward in the classic *Easy-Rider* tradition.

Not only are the best choppers works of engineering art, there's plenty of traditional art in them as well. A paint job on a chopper frame to get the deep rich gloss required by the fastidious rider can need up to 20 coats of the best-quality cellulose, each hand-rubbed down then polished to a super sheen. Then the custom artist goes to work with flowing lines to add that individual treatment so important to the owner.

All possible metal work is brightly plated and some riders even have aluminium engine parts coated with chrome for just that extra sparkle.

The craze has caught on to no great extent outside America, but there it's a boom business with magazines devoted to the cult, and many manufacturers vie with each other for custom for their chopper accessories. And a chopper is not simply a re-vamped old machine. The fan will think nothing of buying a brand-new Honda, then throwing away 90 per cent of what he has just purchased and building the rest into his dream machine.

Films dealing with Hell's Angels and other anti-social motorcycle gangs have gained the chopper cult a bad name, but most road-ridden machines do not fall into the true chopper category. With thousands of dollars invested in his bike, there is no way that the owner is going to use it for occasional trips to a race meeting or to the corner liquor store. He pampers it, wheeling it out only in good weather, and maybe even trailering it to a concourse competition. On high days, such as during the Daytona fortnight, he just parks it in the main street, then stands back to watch heads turn as people pass.

But even the most ambitious chopper fanatic has discovered that there is a limit to what one can do with a motorcycle engine and two wheels. So the cult of the three-wheeler super-chopper has developed. Here, builders take perhaps a six-cylinder Porsche engine, add two enormous 0.3 metre (1 foot) wide rear wheels, the most luxurious padded seat imaginable, and the splindliest front fork and motor-cycle wheel. The result may not be very drivable, but purely as an eye-catcher it reigns supreme.

If America is the home of the custom cult, and California its breeding ground, there is still some chopper activity in other parts of the world, particularly western Europe. But far stricter traffic laws effectively ban far-out choppers although, as many enthusiasts proclaim, their machines are 'built for show – not for go'.

Previous pages: The classic American custom-built chopper with modified engine, altered steering-head angle, extended forks and, above all, a one-off paint and plating job that stamps the machine with the individuality of its owner.

Top right: For some people, the usual kind of paint and modification job is not enough and the way out becomes the far, far out. But, whatever the dream turned into metal becomes, one thing is certain – to take its place in the winner's circle at a custom show, the standard of workmanship must be first class.

Right: There is more than two-week's work in a tank like this and it is obvious that producing a top-class chopper is an expensive business. But many enthusiasts consider the exercise as a worthwhile and highly enjoyable investment.

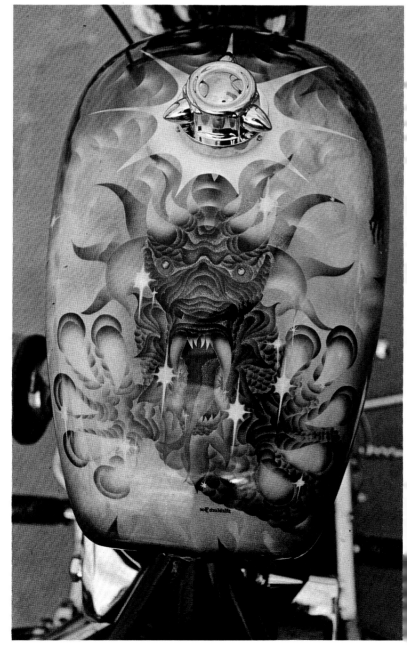

INDEX

Acknowledgments

The publishers would like to thank the following organizations and individuals for their kind permission to reproduce the photographs in this book:

AFIP 42, 65; Associated Press 90; All-Sport (Don Morley) 20-21, 26, 27, 29 below, 32 above, 43, 45, 49 above; Francois Beau 2-3, 56 below, 60 below, 66, 67 above and below; Ian Berry 38; Jacky Broutin 16 below, 17 below left; Gerry Cranham 49 below, 62-63; Colin Curwood 32-33 below; Foto Jan Heese 15 above, 30-31, 36-37, 53 below, 57, 60 above, 61 above, 64 below, 81 above, 82-83, 84, 85 above, 94 above and below; FPG/Alpha 81 below (Thomas Zimmerman) 73; Jim Greening 14, 18-19, 70, 71 below, 74-75; Simon Griffiths 22-23; Hi Torque (Big Bike Magazine) 25, 85 below (Choppers Magazine) 92-93 (Dirt Bike Magazine) 1, 71 above, 72 above and below, 77, 78-79, 80; M. R. Kerley 38-39; Leo Mason 58-59; Andrew Morland 9 above, 11 above, 15 below, 23 above, 86; Motorcycle Mechanic Magazine (Rod Sloane) 30 above; National Motor Museum at Beaulieu 6-7, 8-9 below; Nick Nicholls 10, 11 below, 28, 33 above, 40-41, 44 above and below, 61 below; Mike Patrick 4-5, 46-47, 50-51, 52-53; Pictor International/FPG (Thomas Zimmerman) 54-55; Presse Sports 64 above; Rex Features 16 above and centre, 17 below right, 88-89; Rod Sloane 29 above, 34-35, 91; Spectrum Colour Library 86-87; Tony Stone Associates Ltd 12-13; Syndication International 24; ZEFA 8 above, 48, 76.

PDO 78/243 1:4